ABOUT THE AUTHOR

R. V. Cassill is both a successful professional writer and an experienced teacher
of creative writing. A Midwesterner, he
was born in Iowa, and received his B.A.
and M.A. from the University of Iowa.
At present, he lives with his wife, two
sons and a daughter on a farm outside
Iowa City.

Mr. Cassill's second published story won
an Atlantic "First" contest. Since then, his
short stories and articles have appeared in
many periodicals and have been reprinted
in various collections, such as *The Best
American Short Stories, O. Henry Prize
Stories, New World Writing* and *Fiction
of the Fifties*. He is also the author of a
baker's dozen of novels published in both
hard-bound and paper-bound formats.

At present, Mr. Cassill is teaching in the
Writers' Workshop at the State University
of Iowa. He has previously taught fiction
writing at Columbia University, the University of Washington and the New School
for Social Research.

writing fiction
is an original PERMABOOK edition.

writing
fiction

R. V. CASSILL

A PERMABOOK EDITION published by
POCKET BOOKS, INC. • NEW YORK

WRITING FICTION

Permabook edition published February, 1963
1st printing .... December, 1962

This original *Permabook** edition is printed from brand-new plates
made from newly set, clear, easy-to-read type.
Permabook editions are published by Pocket Books, Inc., and
are printed and distributed in the U.S.A. by Affiliated Publishers,
a division of Pocket Books, Inc., 630 Fifth Avenue, New York 20, N.Y.
*Trademarks of Pocket Books, Inc., 630 Fifth Avenue, New York 20, N.Y.,
in the United States and other countries.

L

ACKNOWLEDGMENTS AND COPYRIGHT NOTICES

I might not tell everybody, but I will tell you.

Walt Whitman

Contents

Contents

Section III: The Concepts of Fiction

Author to Reader

This book is a summary of what I have said in the last twelve years to my classes in fiction writing. What I said to them was what I had learned from my own practice as a writer. These have been years of constant learning for me. Now I know some things about writing that, in the beginning, I had to guess at.

Among the things I know, I am most certain of this—that an apprentice finds in his reading the standards he must meet as a writer. He must always compare his work with the publications of more experienced writers. Therefore I have designed this book to emphasize analytical reading as an integral part of learning to write fiction.

The six short stories included were chosen for variety as well as quality. They are here to serve as illustrations for everything said about the principles of fiction. They can be touchstones for you to use in measuring your accomplishment and progress.

I would advise reading them for pleasure first. It might be better to read them all before you read my first chapter. But that is up to you—left to your convenience and discretion as many other practices will be. I have not attempted to be a drill master; I would rather encourage, as best I can, whatever personal enthusiasms or penchants you begin with.

In any case, you'll find in continuing through my chapters of comment that reading the stories once is not enough. You should return to them often enough to be really familiar with them, so that when we have occasion to examine a few lines from any one of them, you'll recall how that passage is related to the whole story.

Obviously it was impractical to include any examples of the novel, and admittedly there are some crucial differences between the art of the novel and that of the short story. Both are fiction, however. They belong to the same fine family and the analysis of family traits in the short story will be generally applicable to the novel.

The stories were put in the book for your use. Don't treat them delicately. Mark them for reference. Underline examples of technique that you discover in reading them —bits of dialogue, transitions, descriptions, and the like. Fill their margins with notes. Copy them—when and if that is useful as an exercise. Dissect them. Wrestle with them. Make them your own if you want full value from the rest of this book.

Now of course the teacher of fiction writing has more to do than point out successful examples. He has to expound theory and offer practical advice on how to convert theory to practice in the creative act. These are the objectives of the chapters that follow.

I have not prescribed any particular projects to be completed in conjunction with the reading of my text. My assumption is merely that while you're reading you are also working on stories or a novel. I can promise that some of the things I have to say will mean more and will probably be clearer to you if you are actually at work on your own fiction than if you are merely thinking about making a start. I would like to believe the book might still have something to say to you months or years after you first open it, for I have touched on some of the subtlest problems of the art as well as many of the fundamental ones.

In general I attempted to follow a line of progressive complexity, starting with relatively simple matters and ending with the more difficult, but you'll find that the late chapter on Theme returns to the same concerns as the early one on Choosing a Subject. It is not a duplication of the earlier chapter but a more probing examination of the sources of imagination from which the creative act emerges. I make no apologies for this doubling back. It is intentional—and intended to imitate the natural progress of the writer, which must always be cyclic.

As you go on writing you will make an endless series of spirals over familiar landscapes until the familiar at last takes on the wonderful novelty of something you yourself created, something that did not exist before you gave it a fictional form.

I chose to make no special glossary of technical terms or definitions of the principles of fiction. Technical terms have some value, but only insofar as they order our thoughts about the substance of actual stories. So I have let them emerge where they were required for the analysis of various aspects under consideration.

A basic set of these terms—enough to give you a working vocabulary for criticism—will be found italicized in the short notes preceding each of the stories in this book.

If the reader misses among them, or among the chapter headings, some honorable and familiar terms like *suspense, conflict, drama, denouement, complication,* or *pace,* he can content himself that these factors are treated, in one fashion or another, within the text.

I hope that what I have to say may be useful to the writer working alone—as writers must so often work. I hope, too, that it may serve teachers and students of writing who work together in a group. In trying to be as flexible, yet thorough, as I could be, I have included some observations for the beginner and some for the very competent writer. For the latter I would like to put in a caution not to glide too hastily over fundamentals. I think that really accomplished professionals—like great athletes —must return constantly to basic principles, disciplines, and even exercises.

But far be it from me to prescribe close attention to any point after it has been sufficiently grasped. There is something repugnant about doing either mental or physical work for the sake of staying busy. It probably represents an evasion of tasks one is afraid to tackle. And the most valuable part of writing lies in challenging one's secret fears and testing to the utmost one's resources of spirit. It takes courage to write well.

From here on let's try to face frankly the immense and wondrous darkness that every writer, all his life, confronts. The art of language—which includes the art of fiction— is as protean and vast as it is common. No man ever masters it completely. We all swim in it like boys swimming at an ocean beach. Some learn better and more swiftly than others, learning to submit first of all to the nature of the medium, for the best swimmers are those who ally their strength and skill to the properties of water. Fine writers ally their personal imagination and experience to the great imagination of the human race as it is preserved in language and literary forms.

Becoming a good writer is not easy. No process of training can guarantee it. Those who disparage any kind of instruction in fiction writing have a point when they say you can't make a silk purse out of a sow's ear. In my experience, though, it has turned out that very few sow's ears want to become silk purses. Most people who want to write have some correct intuition of fineness in themselves and a correct intuition that learning the disciplines of the craft is a good way to expose and measure that fineness.

I have proposed in this book a number of ideas and a number of ways to work at the composition of stories. It never occurred to me that mere acceptance of the ideas would guarantee any results whatever. I cannot promise to make you into a professional writer or even a good writer. What I do believe—and it is the excuse for this book—is that what I propose may help you organize and effectively advance the talents for observation and expression that you already possess.

The only promise I can make is this: Every increase in the scope of your talent that you earn by responsible work will justify the effort that it cost. Writing is not merely a profession. It is a way of coming to terms with the world and with oneself. The whole spirit of writing is to overcome narrowness and fear by giving order, measure, and significance to the flux of experience constantly dinning into our lives. Out of that din come fear of ignorance, fear of being alone, fear of dying without having defied the brutal indifference of the physical universe. Everyone who writes makes some attempt to face those fears by the very act of writing as best he can.

The writer who sticks loyally to his art and craft has a better chance than most to liberate himself from that apathy that is a prime contemporary symptom of cowardice. He cares. He learns the value of caring by the stewardship of his talent—by following it as it leads him through experience that many people would shun.

So whatever else this book may do for you, I hope it will guide you past the point of being afraid to try—with everything you have, with educated judgment, without hesitation—for success as a writer.

THE

MECHANICS

of

FICTION

1

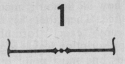

Reading as a Writer

A writer works with his hands. The only proof of his talent lies in the fiction he actually gets on paper. Progress can only be measured by improvement in his manuscripts. No amount of critical insight into the nature of fiction and no amount of colorful experience or vivid daydreaming will spare the writer the trials of getting his story in shape to be read.

But a writer works with his intelligence and his imagination, with observation and judgment, as well as with his hands. Writing is not just typewriting. So before I signal, "Writers, man your machines!" I want to digress for a chapter to explain at length the part that the reading of fiction plays in learning to write it.

If you're awfully impatient to get to work, I can tell you now *exactly* how a story is made. It is made by uttering a declarative statement—"Joe wrote Maureen a dishonest, flattering letter"—and answering the questions naturally provoked by such a declaration: Who is Joe? Who is Maureen? What involvement have they with each other that motivates Joe to write a dishonest letter?

These questions will be answered, obviously, by further declarations, which in turn require explanations. If you

3

keep on giving explanations, presently you will have a story—of sorts.

This is exactly how all fiction is made. In the beginning there is an utterance. Then there is explanation.

However, like any "exact" formula in the arts, this none-too-serious prescription leaves a great deal to be said. To make it serious one must point out exhaustively how a writer learns which questions to ask, how they are best answered, and when enough has been said.

He learns the larger part of what he will ever know about these things from analytical reading. Certainly he may acquire technical principles otherwise than by distilling them from the fiction he reads. And yet, reading remains essential because most technical concepts are learned more quickly and thoroughly from examples than from abstract definitions.

Consider this. It is generally agreed by modern critics and practitioners of fiction that nothing is more characteristic of the art than concreteness of expression. *Concreteness* ought to be your aim in all you write and revise. Very well, you say, but what is this concreteness?

It can be abstractly defined as the rendition of actions, people, places, and things in language that relates how they would be registered by an observer's senses of sight, sound, taste, smell, and touch. Concreteness is about the same as what Henry James called *realization*—the achievement of a sort of evoked reality from mere words.

Such an abstract definition is not without value. But, keeping it in mind, read this passage from Flaubert's *Madame Bovary:*

It was a fine summer morning. Silver gleamed in jewelers' windows, and the sunlight slanting onto the cathedral flashed on the cut surface of the gray stone . . . the square, echoing with cries, smelled of the flowers that edged its pavement—roses, jasmine,

4

carnations, narcissus and tuberoses interspersed with
well-watered plants of catnip and chickweed. The
fountain gurgled in the center . . . bareheaded flow-
er-women were twisting paper around bunches of
violets.

The young man chose one. It was the first time he
had bought flowers for a woman; and his chest swelled
with pride as he inhaled their fragrance, as though
this homage that he intended for another were being
paid, instead, to him.

Note, in the first paragraph, how many senses are appealed to in this realization of a summer morning in a
French city. The gleam of silver and the sunlight on the
cathedral illustrate the visual sensations; the gurgling fountain and the cries of merchants and customers appeal to the
sense of hearing; the flowers and the wet plants stir the
reader's recollection of actual smells.

Then, in the second paragraph, we see a young man in
the midst of this color, sound, and smell. Within the
quoted passage this young man is not described, charac-
terized, or even named. Yet he is as real as fiction can
make him, because here he serves as a focal point for all
the sense impressions set loose by the previous paragraph.
We cannot, of course, quite smell, or see, or hear this
busy city square. (Unlike the theater or the movies, fiction can't rely on immediate sensual impact.) But we are
induced to imagine that the young man is literally assaulted
through every sense—and it is the concreteness of the objective world acting on his mind and emotions that gives
him his fictional reality.

An experienced writer, criticizing the work of an apprentice, is apt to say repeatedly, "Don't tell us what
your character or scene is like. *Show* us." Certainly you
can learn how to *show,* to make your story concrete, by

studying this example from Flaubert. If you return to it twenty times, it will still have things to teach you.

But several examples are better than one. You ought to look for the same qualities of concreteness in the stories in this book. Consider the opening of "That Lovely Green Boat," the descriptions of the fighter and the patrol plane in "The Yellow Raft" and of Anna's home town in "The Lady with the Pet Dog." And don't stop with the examples in this volume. Once you have learned what to look for, all your reading ought to be a search for the variety of technical means by which various writers achieve their ends.

In urging you to read, I am perhaps doing no more than reminding you that a writer has many teachers. Good writers are your real teachers of how to write fiction, and their novels and stories are the means by which they teach. We know that Flaubert "taught" one other writer in a formal sense of the word. He coached, criticized, and advised Guy de Maupassant for several years before allowing him to publish anything. But it is also true that, in a less formal and direct way, Flaubert has taught most of the good writers of the past century—all those who "read as writers" when they looked into *Madame Bovary*.

The last thing I want to recommend is that an apprentice writer become an eager, greedy, joyless brain-picker, rummaging through the libraries of fiction intent on grubbing out only what is immediately useful for his project in hand. There is a fine line to be drawn between emulation, on the one hand, and mechanical borrowing or stealing on the other. I'll try to respect that line and help you define it for yourself even when—for specifically limited objectives—I recommend outright copying or imitation.

In general the analytical chapters to come are attempts to reveal and explain principles that are common to all good fiction, principles everyone is obliged to observe as soon as he learns how to do so.

"Reading as a writer" differs in a number of ways from other readings of fiction.

The ordinary, intelligent non-professional expects, quite rightly, that fiction will give him a kind of illusion that something meaningful is happening to characters who have become very interesting in a particular situation. He recognizes traits of character that resemble those he has observed in life. He finds recognizable values at stake in the action of the story. (Will Joe harm Maureen by his dishonest letter? Will Lambert Strethers achieve magnificence or lose his self-respect?) Whether those values are preserved or destroyed conveys some meaning to the reader about the world he shares with the author. This sort of communication between author and reader is fine. It is the primary justification for fiction.

But there is another sort of transaction going on when a critic pauses to analyze a work. The critic generally wants to determine where to place this particular story. What *kind* of fiction is it? Is it realism or parody or fantasy? If it is realism, is it kin to the realism of Conrad, or that of Dreiser? Does the psychological insight of the story conform to the revelations of Freud? Or is it, perhaps, more intuitive—closer to the intuitions of D. H. Lawrence? Is the style derivative or original? Is the form of the story adequate to the meanings the author tried to load onto it? The critic's way of reading fiction is a good way, too, and a very valuable approach for a writer. If he has time and opportunity, a young writer ought to supplement his writing program with classes in the analysis of contemporary fiction.

When I say that the writer sometimes has to read differently from either the ordinary reader or critic, I don't mean he must permanently change all his reading habits. A writer who is no longer able to respond innocently to the illusion of fiction—as a non-professional can—is in danger of becoming a mere mechanic.

But what the writer wants to note, beyond anything

that concerns even the critic, is how the story, its language, and all its parts have been joined together.

He will look at the way the opening sentences and paragraphs are constructed to put certain information immediately before the reader.

A new person, it was said, had appeared on the esplanade; a lady with a pet dog. Dmitry Dmitrich Gurov, who had spent a fortnight at Yalta and had got used to the place, had also begun to take an interest in new arrivals. (First sentences of "The Lady with the Pet Dog")

There is a watchmaker's precision evident in the form of this opening. The first sentence implies, without a direct statement, that the setting will be one in which rumor has the force of authority, that here people are to some extent free of custom and the rigidity of their family or social position. We will learn from reading farther into the story that Yalta, a resort city, is such a place as is implied. In the atmosphere of transience and rumor, it is common, though a bit odd nevertheless, that ladies should be identified by such superficial trivia as their possession of pet dogs.

The second sentence, which names the principal character, develops our awareness of social fluidity in Yalta by its restrained, wry statement of how quickly one becomes an old-timer in a place where none stay very long.

Thus, from the very beginning Chekhov has begun to develop the peculiarities of the setting in which the love of Gurov and Anna will begin its unworldly flourishing.

Dramatic, concrete, and already ironic, Chekhov's opening draws the reader swiftly into the heart of the experience to be endured by his characters.

Noting the skill of such an opening, the writer who reads it must, *above anything else,* be aware that the story might have opened otherwise. For instance:

In the year 1883, Dmitry Dmitrich Gurov was vacationing at Yalta. His wife and children had remained at the family home in Moscow. While on vacation it was his daily habit to take sweets at a café on the esplanade. The gossips whom he met there one day told him that a new arrival had attracted the attention of many idle vacationers. Her name was not known. They spoke of her as the lady with the pet dog.

The point I wish to emphasize is not that my alternative opening is inferior to Chekhov's—which it certainly is—but that such another possibility for a beginning exists. *A writer reading must be forever aware that the story exists as it does because the author chose his form from among other possibilities.* From this recognition of author's choice comes the key to understanding what is excellent in the fabrication of Chekhov's story or any other good work. Starting from here, you can learn why Chekhov wrote like Chekhov instead of like you.

To the ordinary reader-for-pleasure it ought to seem that the story is told in the language he finds on the printed page because it *has* to be told in just those words. As soon as we know better than that, we are reading as writers.

It is not always easy to understand why the author made the choice he did. For instance, why did Chekhov choose to caricature Gurov's wife as an intellectual shrew instead of picturing her as becoming pathetic as she grows older? That other choice would have served the purposes of the story—but it might have required greater development of her character, thus changing the proportions and center of interest.

We cannot be sure how this other possible choice would have fitted. But mere speculation on it should make us realize that *no choice of character, action, language, names, or anything else is an isolated one.*

Each successive choice made as the writing progresses

has to be made with respect for what has already been established. This is a respect for what I will call the over-all unity of fiction. Suffice it to say for now that when you read as a writer you will keep asking how did the author harmonize A with B and B with C and C with D—on through a very long series of decisions that finally resulted in the story as we have it. We can't understand all the secrets of unifying a story at once. But the recognition of author's choice stimulates a fruitful curiosity. Out of this curiosity, fed by experience with your own writing, analysis, and experience, knowledge of your craft will come at a rate depending on your talent and sweat.

For an example of another particular a writer ought to look for in his reading, let us recognize the obvious truth that characters in fiction have to be developed as the story rolls along. No character can be fully revealed the moment he is brought on the scene. They are developed by encountering situations in which they act to reveal themselves, and act on other characters to affect the outcome of the story.

So one ought to note what sort of occasions in a story extend and amplify the first impressions given of each of the characters. How large an opportunity for character revelation is provided by the particular few situations that constitute any one story?

For a modest approach to understanding how a limited number of situations can reveal as much about character as they do, let's start with a recognition that they were contrived or chosen by the author exactly because of their capacity to expose significant qualities in his characters. We should ask constantly whether another set of circumstances would have served this purpose better or worse. And we remember that in the writing, alternative choices might have been made.

Further examples of what must concern you in your reading:

In most stories that cover any span of time greater than several minutes, we are aware that only a part of the action that might have been given in detail has been fully presented. Why did the author omit some bits of dialogue that might, in actuality, have been spoken? How has the author filled in the gaps that he chose to leave? Has he left some important realities up to the imagination of the reader? Of course he has, unless he is a real bumbler. But a skilled author will have chosen ways to make sure the reader imagined something consistent with what is given, rather than something irrelevant.

And while the author was contriving so many clever joints and putting in so many bolts, hinges, and braces, what else was he doing? Why, he was taking pains to hide all his carpentry work for the sake of the illusion he wants to give the reader.

Perhaps the last thing you need to find out, reading as a writer, is how an author has managed to disguise his own presence, how he has kept the curtain always between himself and the reader.

A writer must read, then, with close concentration. But, it seems to me, a writer ought also to read widely. And what becomes of concentration and close attention to detail when one tries to plunge through a lot of stories, novels, and other reading matter in a short lifetime? Well, obviously there have to be occasions when he reads hastily, avidly, skipping like a stone flung across a pond. There's no need to be afraid this reading is wasted. Thomas Mann's *The Magic Mountain* and James Joyce's *Ulysses* are novels that might reward months or years of concentrated effort. But I suppose it is better (just a *little* better) to have dipped into one or the other during an afternoon's bus ride than never to have opened them at all.

The short stories printed in this book were chosen in the conviction that each, in its own special way, would be worth close examination. Most of them will be referred to in more than one chapter, and that implies you ought to return to each of them for more than one reading. Each time you read, I hope, you'll learn something new.

I have also included a small list of novels in the chapter on the novel. In this case also I recommend them for concentrated reading and a writer's analysis of the means employed to put the thing together. But I do not wish to suggest that this list is sufficient reading to make you into a writer of novels. Go read as many more novels as you can reasonably find time for.

Read drama.

Read poetry. Nowhere are the possibilities of language on display as they are in poetry. Not all these possibilities are suitable for fiction, but the fiction writer ought, by all means, to know that they exist. Furthermore, some of the finest and most subtle narrative forms are found in poetry. Read the English ballads if you don't yet know this is so. (Read the ballads "Little Musgrove," "The Demon Lover," or "Lord Randall" for a tiny sample.) Read William Morris' "The Haystack in the Floods" or "Sir Gawain and the Green Knight" or Robinson Jeffers' "Thurso's Landing" if you want to see how wonderfully stories can be told in verse.

Drama should be useful reading for a fiction writer. Contemporary fiction has borrowed a great deal from the literature of the theater, in form more than subject matter. For economy and deftness in giving information to the reader—for learning how to *show* him instead of telling him what he has to know—we can find worthwhile examples in many plays. Beyond this—it ought to go without saying—means of character delineation have had to be worked out to a high degree of subtlety for the stage.

So read widely. Read good things when you can find them. But don't—if you really mean to master your craft —be afraid of soiling your mind by reading works not exactly of first rank. In my experience, students who purposely confined their college reading to "the best"—meaning Shakespeare, Dante, Cervantes, Dostoevsky, Melville, and Henry James; all great writers, all writers in an idiom no longer common—had more than usual trouble in developing for themselves a supple style that would express their own experience. Sometimes more of one's basic craft can be learned from second rank work.

And now it has occurred to you that I have outlined a reading program that will take years to complete, a reading program with no outside limit. I'm afraid I have. Certainly I do not mean to suggest that all this reading should be done before you put paper in your typewriter and strike out boldly for yourself.

All I expect by now is that you have read this chapter and the story "The Lady with the Pet Dog." Now the next chapter should be the signal to write a story of your own. When you've finished it, read some more fiction.

2

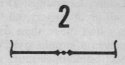

Choosing a Subject

Often in fiction writing classes I have found that the beginning writer will show much better taste and sense in his reading preferences than in the choice of material to be used in his own work. He admires and reads with pleasure the fiction of Hemingway and Faulkner, Katherine Anne Porter and D. H. Lawrence, Stephen Crane and James Joyce—or stories like the ones included in this book.

But lo and behold, when he comes to writing his own first story, some mysterious folly leads him to choose a gaudy, sensational, and unfamiliar subject matter, something snatched from a tabloid or an old-fashioned adventure magazine. Instead of attempting to produce the genuine excitement of discovery that he himself has known in reading good fiction, he hopes to dazzle with the artificial fireworks of exotic situations, cardboard heroisms, billboard beauty and dismaying "surprise endings." (These surprise endings generally depend on the writer's withholding information which should have been given in the first paragraph of the story—that the main character is male, or a baby, or a Negro, or a pet, when the reader has been teased into believing the character a female, a Don Juan, a white person, or merely a human being.)

I never quite understood why students should waste their time and mine on efforts so far off the right track. Sometimes I guessed that they might be afraid to discover how little of their own experience they had actually possessed, how little of their own lives they had grasped.

Certainly it is terrifying to sense that all one's life has flickered away like a landscape seen from a train window, or that what remains from the vanished past is sealed away in memory as if it were in a bank vault for which there is no key. Perhaps it is just a fear of finding nothing in themselves that keeps some intelligent novices from looking at their own lives—and misleads them into using borrowed tinsel and stolen dynamite.

But the choice of becoming a writer is the choice to face some fears, including the fear of being a hollow person, a dull person with nothing to say.

There are many subtle psychological reasons why people do not like to measure themselves. But my best advice —and I cannot state it too strongly—is to face the fear of hidden embarrassments forthrightly and take the subjects for your first stories from your own life.

And don't, please, scan your life for those moments that seem most superficially colorful, nor the moments when more or less accidentally you were cast in the glamorous role of a character from a piece of sensational adventure fiction.

It may well be the case that once upon a time you were involved in a holdup and acquitted yourself like Dick Tracy in the face of danger. It may be that, for the moment, you *were* Dick Tracy instead of your good self. And however entertaining Dick may be in his proper place in the comic strip, he is not a useful character for the kind of fiction I want to encourage. Far better to write about yourself when you were most yourself—in love, and in love with things that vanish, as Yeats puts it.

There are appropriate agencies for rewarding glamorous performances and formal heroism with medals and with cash. Fiction should not attempt to pay tributes to the winners of foot races, those who save orphans from burning buildings, or girls who win beauty contests. In your fiction let heroism or pathos or awe or terror emerge from the homely truth that you have known most thoroughly.

But I am not recommending that, for a beginning, you sit down to turn out a fragment of literal autobiography. Autobiography is a special kind of writing that sometimes has a very high value. It isn't fiction, though, and you ought to plunge with determination into the effort to make fiction.

To make a story out of your own experience, it's almost certain that you'll have to make a *composite* out of bits and pieces of reality gleaned in whatever place or period you can remember them. If you tried to make these pieces stay in the chronological order of your own life, that would be autobiography, properly speaking. In fiction you discard the actual, or chronological, order. The fragments from here and there are put together because they seem—according to the intent of your story—to fit together.

Reality suitable as a subject for a complete story seldom comes to us in single nuggets that require merely to be delivered to the reader in concrete, active, and sensuous prose. But it may be well enough to start writing down a single autobiographical fragment—and then let the composite grow around that.

It is not necessary to see your whole subject before you begin to write. I said in the previous chapter that making fiction consisted in uttering a statement and then answering the questions that naturally arise in an effort to explain it. Your initial autobiographical fragment will serve as the primary utterance. Once a beginning has been made and your memory of a particular circumstance has been exhausted, you'll see the need to fill in the weak or empty or mystifying gaps, to round everything out, to bridge over what memory has lost with memories of *similar,* related things.

It is one of the nice things about writing that the full scope of a subject begins to dawn on one after he starts to write. So once you have a glimpse of the subject, begin to put it on paper. Then, unless stubborn habits of fear and self-doubt are too strong, a flood of memory and imagination will begin. From the flood you will select the materials that show the reader what your subject means—will answer the questions, show the emotional quality of the event and its relation to the universal patterns of loss and triumph that pervade all our lives. Either on your first effort—or your second, or your tenth— it will occur to you that, after all, not much has been lost of anything you ever knew. It has merely been inaccessible, and the act of writing is a way to possess your own life.

If these exhortations to begin, plunge, throw yourself into the deep water of writing a story sound thin and general—and admittedly they are a bit premature; they will be given more substance by later chapters—remember that a writer simply does the best he can at any moment in his development, even when one part of his mind knows he is floundering badly.

But begin you must. If you don't begin until you have all the available theory in your mind, you may never get a story on paper. Moreover, it is three times as easy to absorb theory if you are making efforts of your own to which it can be related.

Not the least of the benefits to be expected by a writer from his reading is guidance in finding his own subject matter.

It must have happened countless times that a writer in the midst of reading has felt a quickening excitement as he realizes, *Something like this—but not quite like this— once happened to me.* His interest in the story before him illuminates some hitherto neglected area of his own experience, suggesting all of a sudden that it possesses an inherent interest that might be exposed by forming it into fiction.

With his memory jogged by someone else's tale—or a poem or a movie—the writer finds himself almost involuntarily flung into preparations for a new story of his own. Most of these impulses will come to nothing and that is all right. The imagination will—and should—make a hundred starts for every story that is carried to completion.

But if the suggestion that comes from reading does prove solid enough to be built on, the odd, nice thing about the process is that the story that emerges need have no great resemblance to the one from which it sprang. No particular effort is usually required to provide for originality in a story that germinated from someone else's effort. The writer may well have intuited a connection between his own proper subject and the one he has been reading about. This subtle relationship will not—in fact it can't—prescribe a similarity in the details of substance and form.

It's been said that there are, fundamentally, only two stories: Cinderella and Jack and the Bean Stalk. It is also said there are less than half a dozen primary myths which are repeated over and over and over in the numberless stories of our culture: the myth of Rebellion, the myth of Salvation, the story of Venus rising from the foam, the Prometheus legend, the triumph of Christ.

Without going into this matter of the universality of a certain few myths that may be built into all stories, we can at least say that, of course, the fundamental pattern of one story may be fleshed out with the concrete details of quite another story.

Look, for example, at the subject matter of William Berge's story "That Lovely Green Boat." Specifically the subject is a summer in the lives of Carl, Helen, Richard Wellman, and "I"—the narrator. They had a splendid, frail green boat which they wrecked eventually because

18

they were too confused with the passions and shyness of early adolescence to do anything better with it.

The subject, seen so specifically, is Mr. Berge's and no one should try to steal it from him.

Seen in a somewhat broader sense, the subject is the frailty of all those promises we try to give each other and ourselves when adolescence begins to waken us. This is my subject—and yours and that of anyone who wants it. There are a thousand ways to tell it. I know how I would tell it. The kind of recollection a writer must, almost perpetually, engage in will surely suggest the way you could tell it—that is, it will suggest a specific subject matter that you may someday use.

Selection of subject matter is an imaginative act. Someone who lacks the fundamental imagination to see that a fist fight on a playground at dusk is more interesting than a group of children numbly watching television shouldn't try to be a writer. It was part of Hemingway's imagination to go to the bullfights in Spain and all the wars he could get to. Legwork is a part of imagination. You've got to go take a look at life, got to have a nose, not so much for news, but for those vital occasions that somehow embody your notion of what our life is like.

Never minimize the importance of selecting your subject. On the other hand don't let your first choice of subject become so difficult that it keeps you from setting to work. Remember that a clear view of one's subject often emerges as one writes, growing fuller and deeper as the writing digs it out of its camouflage. It is not often a mass of ingredients lying ready for assembly on the writer's desk.

In suggesting how reading may point out to us a subject of our own, my illustration was a story about children (or very young people, at any rate). I did not necessarily mean, by choosing this example, to imply that in drawing on your own experience you ought to draw first of all on your experience as a child. A good many writers—and readers as well—balk at the idea of writing about children. "There're too many stories, for Gawd's sake, about sensitive children." It goes without saying that any writer *was* a sensitive child, so there, already, is a very substantial barrier in the way of writing about yourself.

All right then. Don't be moved by any fond and poignant memories of lovely green boats to put down, in a story, the heartache of your fourteenth year. Plunge into experience nearer to your present life and interests.

Remember though that perspective on experience is valuable in getting it into meaningful order. It is often the case that you can be too near a thing to see it whole and steadily. There are certainly handicaps in trying to write about, say, a love affair in which you are presently engaged.

Handicaps exist, then, in choosing almost any part of your experience as an ideal subject, though it remains true that an apprentice should write about people, places, and events he knows well.

Accept the handicaps with the confidence that the subject of your first story need not be the subject of your final masterpiece. Stories about one's childhood may have this advantage—that they lead a writer on to recapitulate in his growth as story teller his former growth as a person. His stories just *may* grow up along with him.

On the other hand, stories written on subjects closer to your present experience may open vistas backward to the rich, potent and definitive revelations which only childhood is privileged to know. A story like "In the Zoo" strikes us as a crowning triumph of adult vision simply because in its ripeness it seems to have mastered the profound riddles that come so early into life. It is fascinating to compare this story with "That Lovely Green Boat." One looks back at childhood. The other looks directly, as if contemporaneously, at it. We can only conclude that each vision has force enough to show the prejudice against stories about children is nonsense.

And in any case, once you have reveled and wrestled with your first subject, doing your best with it, you ought to take a deep breath and admit that it is only a beginning.

A writer must be a strangely divided creature. First he works with blind enthusiasm—then casts a cold, cold eye on what the enthusiasm brought forth. The cold and critical eye is just as necessary and just as much a part of writing as the enthusiasm.

If your cold eye finds that, after all, your first subject was trivial, don't by any means despair of finding in your own experience material great enough for the very highest purposes of the art. Go back again, again, again.

A young writer can hardly help feeling that each story he writes is an ultimate measure of his insight and of what he has to express. Hasn't he been absolutely frank? Hasn't he recklessly committed everything his years have taught him to these pages? Isn't the subject that he has tugged out of his buried life with such anguish and humility all he has of himself to offer a world fully preoccupied with dangers and opportunities? And—that being the case— hadn't he better start looking outside himself for subject matter if he wants to go on writing?

The answer must be *No* to all these questions. What seems ultimate is truly only preparatory. Alps beyond Alps arise, sure enough. The "most important" subject most of us lug out of our youth when we begin to write fiction is usually a pale substitute or sometimes a camouflaging screen for the better subject lurking behind it and beyond it. The search for your true subject will go on long after you have forgotten you read this book.

You cannot possibly see the truth of such a proposition by self-examination at any one stage. The careers of famous writers illustrate it, though, and the one good reason for granting them their fame is that they serve so well as illustrations. (Dear, patient, illustrious dead men. When they were young they never knew about themselves what we know now.)

I think we can see in F. Scott Fitzgerald's earlier novels *This Side of Paradise* and *The Beautiful and the Damned* that he is hunting, still somewhat blindly, for the Jay Gatsby and the Dick Diver who were to be his "real" subjects. The themes, the emotional recklessness, the sense of a precarious social equilibrium, and even the fate of the characters in the earlier books hint that Gatsby and Diver were already lurking in the dark fields of Fitzgerald's imagination, waiting for the writer's stubborn search to "turn the light on them," as he put it once.

The larger accomplishment of Thomas Mann shows about the same thing. All that is unfolded in the great novels *The Magic Mountain, Joseph and His Brothers,* and *Dr. Faustus* is present in embryo in Mann's earlier stories and novels. When they were written, it may very well be that the author felt he had run his imagination to the end of its tether.

So, for the time being, he had. Yet here is the wonderful part of it. Every early choice of subject matter and its exploitation can now be seen as an exploration preparing and conditioning the author to come closer in his next attempt to his true subject.

We see James Joyce in the same way. (Perhaps nearly all great writers.) The subjects of his early stories in *Dubliners*—not to mention the technique and discipline of the language—are surely stations he had to pass through before he was in a position to see Leopold Bloom, the modern Ulysses, as the natural and appropriate subject for a full display of his talents. The novel *Ulysses,* we are told, was originally conceived as one of the series of stories that would make up *Dubliners.* Joyce must have been a little surprised—and happy in the peculiar fashion of writers—to discover he had come home to his true subject in very much the way Ulysses returned to Penelope (or Leopold to Molly Bloom) after many wanderings.

22

The moral here, for you and me, is striking enough. Our cold eye sees, sometimes, that our subjects are of only private importance. As soon as we have learned something about our craft we are tempted to turn from concentration on our own experience to the public world of great events—to write about spies and congressmen. But the first commandment is to go back stubbornly to our own fields. This time—and the next time and the time after that—we must turn them more deeply than before.

In the long run the reward for this may only be that the writer will discover who he really is. His own identity will be clarified as his ability to write of his own experience increases. And that, I think, is a benefit none of us should scorn. That alone ought to entitle writing fiction to a place in the curriculum of the liberal arts.

But beyond that, as one goes on—if he is lucky, stubborn, gifted, and clever enough to learn from partial successes as well as failures—a writer will find that private experience and public experience lose their distinction. The boundary line is rubbed out. At the level of myth they begin to blend into each other, and finally one may discover the common heart of humanity, and hope and doubt and triumph, beating in the subject matter that seemed at first glance to be merely personal experience.

When that happens—and beware! it is not common and never easy—there exists a writer worth everyone's respect, a man in possession of material only he has the privilege to expound.

3

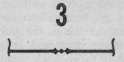

Description, Narrative Passages,
Scenes, and Dialogue

Sometimes when you've done your very best writing you'll feel the impulse to bury your manuscript or turn your back on it and run like a man fleeing the scene of a crime. Sometimes when you've done your poorest you'll want to frame each sheet and hang it on the wall.

Writing is not an impersonal act like adding a column of figures or making a grocery list. It is an act of exposure. If the subject doesn't come from the writer's life, the central emotion does. A writer not yet secure in his craft may very well feel doubly exposed by what he has written. First of all, he has revealed a subject and attitudes that may have been long hidden from the rest of the world. Second, he has, perhaps, exposed his shortcomings as a writer, his inability to shape his material into a story that satisfies his own standards.

No wonder he sometimes disowns, sometimes hysterically overestimates, the value of his effort. That's natural enough, but one can't afford to give in to such feelings often or long. One has to learn to criticize his own work— and then revise. He can't do this very well if he can't read it over without nausea, nor if he convinces himself that a god has given him direct dictation.

The subsequent chapters of this book may provide some useful antidote to a purely emotional appraisal of one's own work. The kind of analysis to be made of stories in this text can lead to enlightened revision. While fear and trembling still disturb your judgment of what you have just written, it would seem profitable to reconsider it with a cold eye on its mechanical characteristics before you pass a definitive judgment on the value ŏf your concepts.

For convenience' sake I categorize the elements of fiction as *mechanical* or *conceptual*. Among the former, I place description, narration, scene, half-scene, transitions, and dialogue. The latter category, to be dealt with later, includes character, plot, tone, theme, and other things less susceptible to mechanical measure.

Different sorts of description and the function of description can be demonstrated pretty well without respect to whether those descriptions are good or bad in themselves. The same is true of other elements I call mechanical. When we talk about character and plot, though, we'll be forced to consider how well they have been conceived if we want to make sense.

DESCRIPTION may be defined as language employed to present directly the qualities of an object, a person, or a scene. The image thus presented is sometimes static, sometimes a transient part of the action of the story.

In "That Lovely Green Boat" we get this description of the boat:

> She was made of thin lath, her bow decked over, and she was painted light green—the color of maple leaves in early spring, and varnished with clear varnish and sanded and varnished and sanded again, and worked on with steel wool until the bottom was as smooth as the granite ice in winter that froze without wind. She was swift and light, like a kingfisher, and she seemed blonde in her greenness.

This is the way the boat would have appeared any time it was looked at. The qualities described are the fixed, permanent qualities of the boat. Yet, even in this description we note that *some* idea of action—of movement and of change—is incorporated into the static image. The bottom is not merely smooth. It has been varnished and sanded and varnished and sanded again. That is, an action or process has been mentioned to enforce the concept of smoothness. So in most good fictional descriptions the static picture is in some way adapted to the movement of the story, the vital progress and change of the characters.

Remember that in the passage quoted from *Madame Bovary* the verbs in the description of the square are mainly verbs of action, though inanimate things are acting and do not change their relationships—as humans would —while we contemplate the scene.

Silver *gleams*. Sunlight *slants and flashes*. The square *echoes* with cries, and the fountains of the French city *gurgle*.

In "The Yellow Raft," where there are many descriptions designed to re-create sense impressions for the reader, the descriptions are hardly distinguishable from the action the story presents.

> In the middle of that afternoon a layer of dingy phosphorescent light disjoined the sea from the sky; then the waves grew massive and took on a solid greenish-black hue, like volcanic glass, each vast undersurface curved and scratched as if by the grinding of pebbles.

The scene itself has been animated by the way the author chose to describe it, and this animation gives a particular sense of the involvement of the man with his environment.

This tendency to integrate descriptions with the other active elements of a story may seem particularly appro-

priate for the purposes of fiction. There is often little excuse for giving the reader more descriptive details than are
required to suggest that the characters are moving in a
world of sound, light, temperature, smell, and taste.

Nevertheless, as the example from Mr. Berge's story indicated, the essentially static image may still serve some
useful purpose. Even in a short story it may be appropriate
to stop dead still for a look at things.

Descriptions may be categorized as concrete, figurative,
and abstract. The distinction among these kinds depends
partly on the language chosen, but also on the way the
imagination of the author has seized on the reality of the
object or person to be described. Nearly every piece of
fiction will contain examples of all three kinds.

In "The Lady with the Pet Dog," we find these concrete descriptions: ". . . the water was a soft, warm lilac
color, and there was a golden band of moonlight on it."
And "The theater was full. As in all provincial theaters,
there was a haze above the chandelier, the gallery was
noisy and restless." And "Directly opposite the house
stretched a long gray fence studded with nails."

These figurative descriptions: ". . . he thought how much
angularity there was still in her laugh and manner of
talking with a stranger." (The word *angularity* is used
metaphorically, suggesting that the figure and movements
of a young girl have their counterpart in her laughter and
manner.) And, in the husband's buttonhole, "there was an
academic badge like a waiter's number." (The simile adds
a note of ridicule to the description of the husband's appearance.)

Abstract descriptions: ". . . in his character there was
something attractive and elusive that disposed women in
his favor and allured them." And "He had two lives; an
open one, seen and known by all who needed to know it,
full of conventional truth and conventional falsehood,

exactly like the lives of his friends and acquaintances, and another life that went on in secret."

Perhaps the main risk inherent in the use of abstract descriptions is that they may pass judgments on characters without allowing the reader to make up his own mind on the basis of evidence. This is called "author intrusion" and can very gravely weaken the sense of reality in fiction. Since concreteness is the soul of fiction, it would seem obvious that concrete descriptions are the safest, the most reliable. It is a good principle to make your reader "see, hear, and feel." Yet it would be foolish to rule out the use of abstract descriptions merely because they *can* be abused.

The kind and number of descriptions we can expect to find in a good story will depend on the author's over-all intentions. There is not an abstraction to be found in "The Yellow Raft" for the very good reason that the author's strategy was to withhold all intellectualized comment on the scene he presents. The reason for this will be given more fully in the chapter on Theme.

On the other hand, a sizable proportion of the descriptions in Chekhov's story are abstract—and this in turn is quite proper because Gurov comes to face the quandaries of love through a series of intellectualized perceptions. The ingredients of morality and reason are fundamental to the meaning of the action here.

The function of descriptions in fiction is generally to deepen the illusion of person and place—to re-create their substance in the imagination of the reader, so that he is willing to believe he is in the presence of reality.

Another function is to mirror the emotional state of characters. The way the objective world is depicted hints at the mood of the people who inhabit it. A crude illustration of this can be given by saying that a description of night, fog, and cold will hint that the characters are miserable or depressed. Descriptions of meadows in May will hint at some bubble of happiness.

Somewhat more delicately shaded examples appear in Chekhov's story. In the first pages we get a description of the sea at Yalta. The sensuous attractiveness of the warm, lilac-colored water and the moonlight playing on it is keyed to Gurov's mood when he first meets Anna. At this time he is careless and indolent—ready to respond to superficial loveliness whether it appears in a human or other natural form.

Later, in the time when the frustrations and contradictions of love have caught him by the throat, it is very natural that his eye might linger (where that of the reader is skillfully directed by the author's description) on the shabby pomp of the provincial theater and the long gray fence studded with nails—a fence gray as the monotony of enforced separation and menacing as the social prohibitions against adultery.

So we see that descriptions of differing quality will serve to emphasize for the reader—like accent marks— the changes that have taken place in the characters and their situation. (A virtuoso performance in using the altering aspects of the exterior world to show the alterations of the psyche is Thomas Mann's *Death in Venice*. There the city in various weathers becomes "mirror and image" of the subconscious changes in the main character.)

Another means of description available to an author consists of having one character describe another. Thus, in "The Lady with the Pet Dog" Anna says, " 'My husband may be a good, honest man, but he is a flunkey!' "

What is accomplished by such indirect description that could not be done better in the author's own words? Certainly the good reader will expect the indirect to be less reliable, more *biased* than the direct.

That's it. The value of indirect description lies precisely in its revelation of bias. The description, as Chekhov uses it, shows the wife's "access of bitter feeling"—and has also given us a view of the husband's character that may be accepted tentatively while we wait for it to be confirmed or refuted.

By shedding some light on two characters—speaker and person he describes—indirect descriptions kill two small birds with one small stone. And in the tight confines of a short story, the writer has to search constantly for ways to achieve economy.

Further, this sort of indirect description contributes to the lifelikeness of fiction. Frequently we hear about people before we meet them and have a chance to judge them for ourselves. By what we hear we are predisposed to like or dislike them. Then when our own direct impressions of these people force us to a reappraisal of expectations, we find ourselves at the point of conflict between authorities. However mild that conflict may often be, it is the very stuff of drama. Much of the celebrated "dramatic" method of Henry James is an exploitation of the conflict between expectation and discovery.

TRANSITIONS. Since the texture of fiction ought to be consistent, and a story ought to progress with a smooth flow from one passage to the next, you will want to watch for the means various authors use to move from description to narrative, from narrative to scene.

To move from a static description, the classic transition is provided by having someone act on whatever has been described. (If the author has described a melon, someone cuts a slice out of it. If he has described a pool, someone dives into it. After which, Someone becomes the center of interest.)

You might turn back once more to the passage from *Madame Bovary*. Note that the transition from description to action is made by having the young man enter the square and choose a flower from one of the flower stands. After the stillness of the picture is disturbed, the author can proceed smoothly to telling us about the young man and about how he feels.

Note how in the fourth paragraph of "That Lovely Green Boat" the transition is made from the description of the boat to the narrative of action in which the three children are involved that summer. The boat has been fixed, statically, in our mind's eye. The picture begins to live and move when we see the three of them coming down to the boat and rowing it out into midstream.

Is it too fanciful to say that the reader's imagination is in this way transported into the midstream of the story, ready now for what will happen?

NARRATIVE PASSAGES are those parts of fiction which condense action into its largest movements. They are long-range views in contrast to the detailed close-ups of action and characters given in scenes. Narrative passages may telescope the events of several years into a few small paragraphs or less, while the time it takes to read a full scene is roughly comparable to the time it would require to be enacted.

There is no end to the variety possible in the composition of narrative passages. The examples given here are not intended to illustrate the full range of possibility, but only to fix general characteristics in your mind. Henceforward in your reading of fiction, be on the lookout for varieties of usage. You'll find there is a special pleasure —as well as advantage—in an awareness of the mechanical design in fiction.

In "The Lady with the Pet Dog" the first several paragraphs of Section III constitute an uninterrupted narrative. The constant and repeated experiences of several months are depicted as a single bloc of action from which emerge no specific occasions having anything to do with the center of interest. We are told that the image of Anna did not fade as Gurov had expected it to. We are *not* given an instance of his summoning that image to mind or re-

31

living his memories in detail, though such an instance might have had considerable dramatic force. The realism of the story would not have been violated by its inclusion. But the principle of economy probably ruled it out.

Since economy is nearly always an issue in the short story, we can see why the compression of time and action into narrative passages may often be useful. The novel doesn't impose such strict demands for economy, but there the choice to present certain things in narrative may be used to change the pace, to subordinate the sequences of lesser interest, and to summarize when the reader has already been given all the detailed views he needs.

The narrative of Section III serves—as narrative passages usually do—as a bridge between the scenes at Yalta and the scenes in the provincial town to which Gurov goes in search of Anna. The routine of this protracted period is given considerable concreteness even though the view is a long-range one. "When the first snow falls, on the first day the sleighs are out, it is pleasant to see the white earth, the white roofs; one draws easy, delicious breaths. . . ." "When in the evening stillness the voices of his children preparing their lessons reached his study, or when he listened to a song or to an organ playing in a restaurant, or when the storm howled in the chimney, suddenly everything would rise up in his memory. . . ."

The author has managed to compress time without abandoning concreteness. He does this by choosing for the passage sensuous details that are recurrent through the period he is telling about. He has also adapted his verbs and time modifiers to express the sense that rich and detailed life is going on, though so far away from our point of observation that we can only guess at the vast majority of details.

While narrative passages generally appear as links between the more scenic parts of a fictional work, they also serve sometimes to get a story started. In the long perspective of narrative we are given the main outlines of a situation and an action that has been developing over an extended period. Then, when the author has satisfied us that the action is approaching a climax, he shifts to closer range and the illusion thenceforward is that we are observers at the scene itself. So narrative may also be thought of as a transitional phase preparing the reader's interest until he is ready to accept the illusion of a pure scene. It conditions him, sometimes, for a "willing suspension of disbelief" by requiring, first of all, only as much suspension as is necessary to accept some generalized information about the way human affairs commonly run.

In any case, narrative passages normally progress into scenes. Section III of the Chekhov story begins with narrative, moves on into a scene.

The transition is marked by the words "One evening. . . ." That means, in the sense of the story, "on one of those evenings that altogether have constituted the whole period covered by the preceding narrative." It is a mechanical signal to the reader that now we are going to get down to the scene itself and he had best be ready to accept the illusion of being an observer.

It is, for our taste today, a bit too obviously mechanical. It is by no means wrong to use such a signal, but smoother transitions may avoid drawing the reader's attention to the carpentry of the story.

Consider this narrative passage and the transition at the end: (From George P. Elliott's "Sandra")

I did not realize fully how much I had come to depend on her until she fell sick. She was in the hospital with pneumonia for three days and spent six days convalescing. It was at Thanksgiving time. I declined invitations out to dinner, in order to keep Sandra company—to tend to her, I said to myself, though she tended to herself very nicely. I was so glad to have her well again that the first time she could come to me I kept her in my bed all night—so that she might not chill herself going back to her own bed, I told myself. That was the first time, yet by Christmas we were sleeping together regularly, though she kept her clothes in her own room. She still called me sir, she still washed my feet; according to the bill of sale I owned her; I thought her a perfect slave. I was uneasy no longer.

In fact, of course, I was making a perfect fool of myself, and it took Helen to tell me so.

"Dell," she said over the edge of her cocktail glass, "you're in love with this creature."

Evidently there is a great deal of "subject matter" here that might have been expanded into scenes or at least given some more detailed treatment. The illness, the recovery, the comic pretense of solicitude as an excuse for bringing the slave back to her master's bed—all of this *could* have been inflated. I think we have to assume that the author presented it in just this narrative form to keep the proportions of his story true. If this material were expanded, interest would have been diverted from something else. Yet, if it were omitted, the continuity of the relationship would have been falsified.

Note that the last two very short paragraphs manage the transition from a running narrative in the author's words into the dialogue of a scene without recourse to such set-changing tags as "One evening when Helen was having cocktails with me she said . . ."

The single detail of the cocktail glass is all the signal we get—and all we need—of the change.

Scenes in fiction bring the action and sometimes the dialogue of the characters before the reader with a fullness comparable to what a witness might observe or overhear if he had been present. Usually the scenic parts of a fictional work can be located by flipping casually through the pages until the eye catches the marks indicating dialogue.

(Note that there is no dialogue in "The Yellow Raft," yet it consists almost entirely of small scenes linked into tight unity by the narrative passages. As a whole the piece gives the effect of a single, protracted scene. The unusual absence of dialogue in a scenic work is one of the reasons for including it among the stories in this book. It represents an uncommon technique—and is an uncommonly good story.)

While scenes bring to the reader an amplitude of detail comparable to that of reality, a moment's reflection tells us that comparison can only reveal an illusion. Prose simply cannot catalogue all the details that would be recorded by a movie camera. It can, however, select and emphasize a crucial pattern of detail as no camera ever could.

The composition of a short story is a constant juggling act, with the author trying always to give the effect of fully reported scenes while still keeping them as brief as possible. The stories in this volume show various ingenious compromises between fullness and economy, and perhaps we must say that none of them represents perfection. A scene is, by its nature, a compromise and it is illogical to call any compromise perfect.

But indeed there can be splendid compromises. A very considerable part of the aesthetic pleasure we get from reading fiction comes from appreciation of the virtuosity evident in the design of scenes.

Stories that open with scenes have some definite advantages over those opening with narrative or description. They immediately catch the reader's interest by the direct encounter of characters and the sensuous detail of movement. They have the corresponding disadvantage—the reader has not been prepared to see what is significant in the profusion of scenic detail. An opening scene can bewilder the unprepared reader and set up expectations that the story will not fulfill.

This risk is not ordinarily a grave one. What is not fully clarified in the opening passages of fiction will normally be made to disclose its meaning by what follows. Every reader knows a story can't be blurted out as instantaneous revelation. If you have roused his interest by a dramatic opening, he is usually content to read on and see what the encounter meant.

Of the stories in this book "The Best of Everything" and "In the Zoo" begin scenically and then move into flashbacks that fill in the story of what has gone before. The scene that opens "In the Zoo" (the two sisters watching the grizzly bear and noting his resemblance to Mr. Murphy) has no particular dramatic tension of its own. It provides, merely, a sort of neutral ground from which the narrator may survey the conflicts of the past. It is not extraneous to the story, however. The full meaning of the action that took place so long ago can only be revealed by showing the blights and pangs that have carried over into this peace. It functions as a sort of magnifying glass to expand the scale of some superficially trivial anguishes —thus giving a tragic dimension to what might have seemed merely pathetic without it.

"The Best of Everything" though, opens scenically in the middle of the story. The day before Grace's wedding is not the beginning of her involvement with Ralph—that beginning will be told in a flashback after the scene has established the characters—but it is the start of a present, unified action that will terminate with his visit to her apartment. This story is a good example of the kind that begins "in the middle of things." It is worth studying for its fine scenic construction and for the smooth, deft use of a flashback.

Note well that while the flashback represents a movement backward in time, it actually advances our knowledge of the characters introduced in the preceding scene. It comes in at just the moment necessary to answer some of the questions presented by the scene. (Why is Grace going to marry a man so different from herself? A man whom, in her terms, she hardly even knows?)

Both of these stories that begin with scenes illustrate another cardinal principle of using flashbacks: Make sure that something has been developed in the present scene to waken the interest of the reader. Create some degree of suspense before you move back into the past. Nothing is so out of place as a flashback stuck into a story before the reader knows why he ought to care about what happened before.

Sometimes a short story consists of a single scene, resembling a one act play. There are several fine Hemingway stories of this kind, and since you owe it to yourself to know the work of this modern master very well, I can hardly do better than to recommend here that you read his collected stories—with admiration and a shrewd writer's eye—for the way they reveal character and economically yield the meaning of the action.

Most commonly, though, more than one scene is required to round out a story. That is true of all the stories in this book ("The Yellow Raft" partly excepted).

I recommend a close look at "That Lovely Green Boat" to find what may be accomplished by a series of closely related scenes in the body of a story. You will see that these permit a progressive revelation of character as well as an advance through the complications of action.

Note also how the scenes are linked together in a series. At the end of each one a few threads are left dangling—either some unbalance of emotion that must be restored later to equilibrium or some practical question about the boats that may be answered in subsequent scenes.

The purpose of a scene at, or very near, the end of a story is to provide an occasion for the showdown between whatever forces have been in conflict through the body of the action. Such a showdown scene is sometimes referred to—in fiction as well as in the drama—as an "obligatory scene." It is obligatory in the sense that when one fighter says he can lick another he must stage a test encounter to see if he is right. Another example might be found in the conventional Western story where the rustler claims he can beat the sheriff to the draw. They have to shoot it out to determine which is faster. A scene permits the reader some degree of illusion that he is present when the showdown comes.

Is it obligatory to end stories with an "obligatory scene" —with a dramatic resolution the reader has been led to expect? There is no final answer. Many fine stories are concluded with such scenes. Some are not. The principle that must be respected is that every story must have *some* resolution, some denouement, whether this is accomplished scenically or otherwise. Chekhov said once that if, in the opening passages of a story, the author mentions a gun hanging over a mantelpiece, the story isn't properly finished until that gun has been fired. A climactic, "obligatory" scene obviously offers a good chance for someone to shoot it off.

It might be useful to you to compare the number of scenes, their length, and their relation to linking passages of narrative in each of the stories in this book. You'll find that the structure is different in each. Each one was built according to the requirements of the subject. There is no such thing as an ideal mechanical form that could be imposed with equal propriety on different kinds of material.

Note that there is also variety among the scenes of any one of the stories. Not all are the same length. Not all of them are intended to focus the reader's interest on the same sorts of things.

"Sandra," for example, contains a few rather fully developed scenes, complete with dramatic dialogue. But we also find this miniature:

One evening six months ago, I came home to find no dinner cooking, no foot bath waiting for me, no sign of Sandra in her room. I found her lying on my bed reading *McCall's* and smoking with a jewel-studded holder I had given her when she was my wife. She flicked an ash onto the rug when I entered the room, waved a languorous *Hi!* at me and kept on reading. I had my choice; she had clearly set it up for me. I hesitated only a moment. I went down to the basement where I had stored away the three-tongued lash which had been provided along with the manual of instructions when I had first bought her, and I beat her on the bed where she lay.

Not only is this brief. It is bare of color and dialogue. But it has all the ingredients of a scene. It permits the significant encounter of two characters. A decision is forced before our eyes. And the episode shown has a sort of completeness in itself, within the larger whole of the story. It might also be said that as a change of pace this abbreviated scene is elegantly adjusted to the more fully extended ones and to the narrative passages.

But, though scenes may be brief and bare, nevertheless it is pertinent to distinguish "half-scenes" from even the most skeletal of genuine scenes.

A HALF-SCENE is essentially an integral part of a narrative passage. It is an interruption of pace, not a shift to another kind of presentation. It is not intended to be complete in itself. It is clearly subordinate in significance to the passage of narrative in which it is placed. It might be thought of as mere relief to the eye of the reader, tired from a prolonged passage of narrative.

But it is more than that. It is a momentary shift from

a distant view of the subject to a close-up, not designed to present a dramatic resolution but to borrow some of the qualities of the scene for a sample—as if to show what the narrative is really talking about.

· A great deal of Chekhov's fiction is scenic in quality, even when true scenes are used sparsely. His wonderful long story "My Life" offers such a dexterous use of half-scenes that one almost imagines himself to be reading a series of scenes from one of Chekhov's plays. Actually, narrative makes up the bulk of many sections of the story.

From "The Lady with the Pet Dog" I'll extract one example for illustration. In Section III of that story there is narrative exposition of Gurov's desire to share his memories of Anna with someone. In the very midst of this exposition comes the transition into scenic presentation.

Gurov says to an official with whom he had been playing cards:

> "If you only knew what a fascinating woman I became acquainted with at Yalta!"
>
> The official got into his sledge and was driving away, but turned suddenly and shouted:
>
> "Dmitry Dmitrich!"
>
> "What is it?"
>
> "You were right this evening: the sturgeon was a bit high."

That's all we're given of this encounter between two men, and we realize that in and by itself it has not accomplished the things we expect of a scene. The narrative resumes immediately to explain Gurov's indignation at the general crassness around him which frustrates even his wish to share memories. The narrative tells us more than the inserted dialogue shows us. But the little exchange has given us a sudden, stunning insight into what the narrative is actually referring to. It's a sample set in to throw its ugly light on the whole complex period covered by the narration.

A half-scene will not do the job that scenes can do in advancing the story line or permitting characters to reveal themselves. But it will, properly handled, lend some of the emotional directness and liveliness of scene to extended passages of narrative.

DIALOGUE is a fundamental ingredient of most scenes or half-scenes. Beyond this, we ought to recognize that it is such a useful technical resource it deserves study and practice in its own right.

More than anything else, perhaps, good dialogue brings a sense of life to fiction—of life precisely observed and candidly re-created. The great fictional requirement of concreteness is satisfied by dialogue as by few other resources at a writer's command, because the reader is permitted to hear the characters of a story speaking in their own voices, revealing the most delicate shades of personality and interest by what they say or ask.

Poor dialogue, on the other hand, gives away the writer's ineptitude more quickly and more devastatingly than any other fumbled passages of his story. He can tell us that his chief female character is witty, lively, and cheerful. And we are likely to believe him, up to a point. But if the girl then speaks like a stupid, conventional frump, no amount of persuasion by the author will convince the canny reader that she is anything else.

Our first demand on dialogue, then, is that it should conform to character and be natural. (Even in a fantasy or other highly artificial kinds of fiction this simple principle will hold. If characters speak in fantastic situations and fantastic environments, their speech ought to sound native to such situations or settings.)

There is, alas, no way to teach anyone to write natural-sounding dialogue. Concentration in reading good dialogue will help—but only if one uses what he learns from read-

ing as a guide to listening to the way people talk in real
life. The fundamental truth remains: You must learn by
listening.

The playwright Synge is supposed to have bored a hole
in his floor so he could listen to the maids gossiping in
the kitchen below. He was on the right track. But eaves-
dropping is perhaps not the primary tactic. You can listen
as well to the people with whom you talk in the course of
each day. You'll detect peculiarities in the way each person declares himself—volubility, reticence, syntax, vocabulary, emphasis, emotion, degree of intelligence, degree of
interest—all these characteristics are detectable in every
conversation. Learn to measure them as a step toward
reproducing them when your fiction requires it.

More than this (and easier, too, I should think)—get
the habit of listening to yourself. Naturalness in fictional
dialogue requires that a single character should express
himself differently according to the circumstance in which
he finds himself. You don't sound the same when you
crawl sleepily and anxiously out of bed in the morning
as you will later in the day when your roommate pawns
your typewriter. Whether you know it or not, you use a
monstrous variety of voices in carrying on your everyday
life. What do all these voices say?

Listening to yourself, learning your own voices, will pay
off splendidly when you have to invent dialogue. In creating a scene you have to become something of an actor.
Confronted with a particular situation, what would you
say in the place of your character? If you know what you
would naturally say in his predicament, you can probably
approximate natural-sounding speech for him. Then you
can tinker with the approximation like a piano tuner
among the strings until you've given the speech its exact
and proper note.

Ordinarily it is a mistake to try to reproduce dialect by
phonetic spelling. And if you concentrate more on the
peculiarities of a character's speech than on its common

qualities, you are more apt to caricature him than to bring him alive. Only one story in this book—"The Best of Everything"—exploits the special speech patterns of its characters by distortions of spelling. " 'Whaddya—in a hurry a somethin?' " says Eddie. Ralph says, " 'Wha' happen ta you, wise guy?' " In this story there is probably a good reason for such a practice. The difference between Grace's sensibility and Ralph's—revealed by different manners of speech—adds poignancy to their mistake in thinking they can marry.

Nevertheless, such distortions ought to be used very sparingly, and when there is no overwhelming indication that they are needed, they are apt to annoy the reader more than they can enlighten him. Note that a great many of the effects Mr. Yates achieves in his dialogue come from imitating the vocabulary and syntax of Ralph and Eddie rather than from phonetic spelling. " 'Ah, you don't want the roommate, Eddie. The roommate's a dog. A snob, too, I think. No but this *other* one, this little *Gracie* —boy, I mean, she is *stacked.*' "

We recognize this as Ralph's true and natural voice, though every syllable is spelled correctly.

Try reading passages of dialogue aloud. Can you hear the difference between the voices in "That Lovely Green Boat"? In "In the Zoo"? Sometimes the variations among speakers are very slight, but in the whole body of the story they ought to be clearly detectable.

Some stories consist mainly of dialogue. They are hardly to be distinguished from plays, and in almost any fiction that employs extended passages of dialogue some of the tactics of the dramatist will be used. That is, dialogue will give information (according to the bias and knowledge of the speakers); it will demonstrate the conflict of emotions; and it will advance the action of the plot. If "That Lovely Green Boat" did not have so many shifts of scene, it might be converted into a play by extending the dialogues already in it.

At the same time, it is well to remember that in fiction dialogue is never a truly independent element. What the characters say must always be related to the author's or narrator's prose, as the various notes in a chord of music are related without dissonance. The dialogue in a half-scene, for instance, will express something a bit different from the narrative prose around it, but the difference can only be a modulation. It must not contradict what the author is trying to get across. And while, sometimes, a fragment of dialogue may be used to give emphasis to some point, at other times the amount of significance in a speech will be emphasized by its immediate context of narrative prose.

" 'If you ever come back here again, I'll kill you!' roared Mr. Murphy. I think he meant it, for I have seldom seen an anger so resolute, so brilliant, and so voluble."

This small example illustrates the interdependence of dialogue and narrator's explanation. The direct quotation certainly reveals Mr. Murphy's anger. *But* the following sentence is required to fit this anger firmly into the story. We all know that people sometimes say things they don't mean. It is one of the resources of dialogue that it can give voice to the extravagances of a windbag or an unguarded tongue as well as the shyness or reticence of another kind of character. Dialogue extends the range of the vocabulary and the emotional tone of one's prose. Still the counterpointed relationship between this extensive range and the limited, reliable observation of the story teller is more important than either by itself. The counterpoint permits grace, precision, and fullness of a sort not to be found in a printed play.

Dialogue must sound natural and its significance must be keyed to that of the story as a whole. Beyond this, we need to remember that it is, nevertheless, an element of fiction that may be called mechanical. It is an artifice.

Conversations in stories do not reproduce those of actual life. They must be structured to fit fictional requirements.

This following fragment may indeed sound like natural speech. It is also very shrewdly manipulated and arranged.

A brown-haired boy about as old as Carl held the boat to the dock and in a voice just a cut above normal talking said, "Do you want a ride?"

He said it in the way a man with five dollars offers to loan you a dollar just to show you he's got money and can afford to borrow out.

"No thanks," I said. "We got boats of our own."

"I see you have," he said, as though I had been trying to explain to him an arithmetic problem he had solved the year before. "You got a motor for that green boat?"

"Don't want a motor," I said. "Rowing, she stays on the water. With a motor, she'd fly."

"Do *you* want a ride?" he said again, nodding his head toward Helen.

"I told you once—"

"I don't mean you, I mean your sister."

"He's not my brother," Helen said. She didn't even look at me when she spoke.

"Do you want a ride?" the boy said again.

"No she doesn't want a ride," I said.

"Yes, I'd like a ride," Helen said, as though she had just been awakened for breakfast.

"Wait a minute, Helen, you don't even know his—"

But she was running down the dock. . . .

Note that: (1) The interspersed observations of the narrator—even "he said" and "she said"—have been placed to provide pauses in the interchange of words, to establish a cadence to the conversation. This uneven cadence indicates shades of reluctance, brashness, and antagonism. The emergence of Helen's eagerness to go with the stranger is demonstrated by the gradual increase in directness and frequency of her speeches.

(2) The question, "Do you want a ride?" is repeated three times. By this structural device the author has demonstrated the rudeness and single-mindedness of the stranger. Further, each repetition has a slightly different inflection given it by its immediate context. These different inflections of an unchanging question show the progress of hostility, measured by the yardstick of an unaltered intent.

(3) The relation between the direct quotations and the narrator's thought has been carefully managed to suggest that much more is going on in the minds of all three characters than can be, or need be, stated. This is an achievement of economy and intensity beyond anything we would get from speech that merely satisfied the requirement of sounding natural.

In building passages of dialogue, remember that any statement or question may draw a variety of responses. Frequently an indirect response gives a more natural effect than a direct one.

Suppose, for instance, that one character addresses another in this fashion: "Is your girdle too tight?"

The direct answer would be "Yes," "No," or "Not really."

But how much more lifelike if the lady so addressed responds, "Let me out of here! Stop the elevator! Let me out of here!"

Even better, she might answer, "I was on my way to shop for a spring suit."

The indirect response is often better because it conforms to the fact that dialogues in actual life are often two or more interrupted monologues. Two minds are seldom operating on the same wave length. Therefore the answer that A has in mind when he asks a question is not always the answer that B is stimulated to give.

In the last example above, it would seem that the lady questioned is merely reminded, by the question, of her reason for putting on the tight girdle in the first place. Her mind is shown spinning on its own orbit, merely tangential to that of the questioner. And so it often is in reality.

As a rule of thumb, we might say that direct response in dialogue is more appropriate when the objective situation fuses the interest of the speakers.

So, when a lion is approaching and one hunter says to another, "Is your gun loaded?" the second would, in all probability, say "Yes" or "No."

Indirect response reveals the mental gulf between speakers when each is busier with his own thoughts than with the superficial subject of the conversation.

Two men are having drinks before catching a train for home. One says, "My boss was on the warpath today." The other replies, "I forgot to buy the birdseed Beulah asked me to bring."

Modulation from the direct to the indirect and back is a means of control over passages of dialogue. It permits a range of exposure extending from the purely superficial to the profound.

Dialogue serves a definite, though limited, purpose in providing a change of pace in extended passages of narration. The reader's eye welcomes the novelty in lines set off by quotation marks.

Also, when one speaker has a great deal to say— several paragraphs of information, perhaps—the interspersal of comments from the persons listening to him will serve as a reminder that they are still on the scene.

These usages are of no great importance. They are no

more than mechanical practices. But, of course, the careful writer will concern himself with every aspect of his work. He will always remember that the mechanics of fiction are among the resources with which he must work his magic.

4

Finger Exercises

It is most annoying—but often true—that the writer who needs discipline most has had the least opportunity to acquire discipline over himself or discipline over his method of writing.

A time will come for you when you can work every day, when each day's work will flow on smoothly from what you did the day before, and when you no longer labor under the anxiety that every paragraph is leading you farther off from what you intend to say. It takes time, we say sagely, to acquire the good habits and the confidence of a professional writer. Don't worry. If writing always remains hard work—and it will, to the very end—at least some aspects will become easier as you gain experience.

The only catch in this comfortable advice is that the confidence of the professional writer is apt to come when it is no longer so grievously needed. It is the apprentice writer, the beginner, the earnestly struggling young talent who needs the confidence—and the means to bolster it. There is a kind of brutal mockery in saying to such a one that experience will ease his path. How is he going to get usable experience as a writer when, at this writhing moment, he is stuck, stuck, stuck?

Well, he can sweat out the frustrations of his early efforts, learning by trial and error. Good men have done that before him, some of the best. And the courage to take his lumps and still go on trying always to do better is a good test of whether he seriously wants to be a writer.

Yet, of course, any teacher worth his salt believes with all his heart in the shortcuts that will save his students some of the pains of learning by trial and error. He will propose every expedient he can think of to get his student past the hurdles and into the open stretch.

The teacher of writing knows that sometimes the most promising young writers are frustrated to the point of rage and brought to a standstill by the discrepancy between their intentions (which are clear enough to them) and their performance in writing (whose shortcomings are just as clear). That is the time when orthodox *and* unorthodox suggestions are called for to get the stalled talent in motion again.

In most of the other chapters of this book the suggestions and advice are roughly orthodox. I have the feeling that the "finger exercises" I have to recommend here may be a little suspect to the true believers in the art of writing. But against that I lay my stout conviction that they can sometimes help.

I don't want you to keep butting your head against the stone wall of technical problems that are beyond your present means to solve. I'll admire anyone who does that —and gets groggily to his feet, lowers his bloody head, and runs again. But I know there's a law of diminishing returns in such blind gallantry. I have a notion that there may be exercises which, sometimes, may point a way around or over the wall.

But before describing some exercises that can be helpful, let me state one thing clearly: Whatever is produced as an exercise has no value in itself. It is a means to a desirable end. That is all. Absolutely all. Your waste basket is the right and proper destination for everything you turn out as an exercise.

Now the exercises.

First, since the next-to-last chapter involved you in thinking about descriptions, bits of narration, and scenes, it seems that it might be useful to write a number of each of these story fragments.

Practice short, medium, and long descriptions. Remember that the grand objective in any description is to distinguish a particular and concrete thing from all that resembles it. When Flaubert was coaching young de Maupassant, he told him to go watch the cab drivers in front of a Parisian railway station and practice describing *one* of them in language that would single him out from all the rest hanging around there.

Obviously more than the use of language is involved in such practice. It is also an exercise in observation, in the selection of significant details from the multitude of common ones. (All French cab drivers have red noses and greedy eyes—but *only one* sits in his cab with the peculiar poise of a man driving a racing sulky at a provincial fair.)

In practicing fragments of narrative, the observation of striking particulars won't help much. It is not the nature of narrative to depend greatly on detail. Rather, in such exercises you ought to test your power to generalize and summarize an extensive action or period of time.

"After six tedious months of training at Camp Vandiver, my regiment embarked from San Francisco. . . ." And then? What was the quality and general content of the next six months? Of the month after that? And the following week? And of the morning just before the adjutant stabbed the Colonel?

Answer the general questions following from some such statement as I gave in quotes, and you have a narrative

51

passage. All you need now is a story in which to use it . . . No? Try another practice shot. Another. Everything you put on paper—if you do it conscientiously—helps you get the feel of the medium in which you have chosen to work. Write *something* every day, even if it must remain a homeless fragment, doomed to the waste basket. Write it as well as you possibly can.

In practicing scenes it may be good training for you to go from some scene in your daily, normal life straight to your writing desk and (1) put down *everything* you can remember of the setting, the appearance of the people in it, their actions and their dialogue; or (2) try to make an economical selection from all you remember and form it so that it will convey the essential quality of the scene as you felt it.

Again, in such practice, you are testing your powers of observation and recall. The more you demand of them, the more valuable the exercise.

But remember—when you're getting pretty cocky about your capacity to hold a great deal in a photographic memory—that a writer doesn't and shouldn't observe in the same way a camera or tape recorder would. As a general principle it is better to observe as a participant than as a bystander. Even though the participant in a scene misses some detail that a bystander might note, active, wholehearted participation requires that the emotions work automatically to select what counts from the noise that doesn't. For purposes of practice in writing scenes it is probably better to write of an occasion when you've quarreled with your girl than of one in which you have, from the sidelines, watched a crueler man beat *his* girl with a chair leg and then defy the police who came after him.

I know a writer who talks a lot—in fact, shouts a lot—at parties, and yet he has the uncanny ability to hear, over the sound of his own voice, all that really characterizes the commotion around him. He may be socially boorish, but as a writer he knows what he's doing. I guess he's using his loud voice as a kind of screen to keep insignificant detail out of his consciousness—and to draw unguarded responses from those he tempts into argument with him.

I also want to propose some exercises of imitation. That word—*imitation*—will sound simply horrid to many writers and to the very best of the inexperienced ones. What? you'll say. Imitation? If I can't at least be original, then writing is a pure waste of my time. Besides, it isn't fair to copy someone else. . . .

Now of course it is cheating to imitate anyone else's work and try to pass the result off as your own contribution to literature. Who said you should try to pass it anywhere except into the incinerator?

To anyone who truly fears that a little indoor imitation will set him in a rut he can't break out of, or set his foot on a path that will lead inevitably to embezzlement and counterfeiting U.S. currency, I must say, for heaven's sake, don't do it. But I strongly believe that those with enough equanimity to try a few imitations now and then will learn something about their craft that can hardly be learned so quickly in any other way. It is only to them that the following comments are addressed.

By now you have read the short stories in this book at least once and have, I hope, returned to them either for rereading or for examination of certain special elements in them. They offer a very large body of material from which you might select, for imitation, passages that have particularly impressed you.

Let me simply show, by imitating the first three paragraphs of "The Best of Everything," how you should go about it:

Some of his friends thought George might go on a rampage the day after his wife left him. As a precaution, two of them stayed overnight at his house, though he had not asked for company.

A crumpled note lay among the unwashed plates on the kitchen table—from Miranda, his wife—and the three short sentences in Miranda's careful script explained sufficiently why she had gone home to Monterey. Miranda had considered their marriage a hollow mockery since she found out about the girl in the beach house at Carmel, and yesterday when she confronted him in tears, he had turned his back on her, busying himself with some unnecessary repair work, whistling and refusing to answer her accusations.

"Got to get this rain gutter mended, Miranda," he had said. "Bad weather coming. Why don't you go shopping and forget about *that?*"

Now, with the text open beside you for constant reference, write your own imitation in three exactly parallel paragraphs. If such an exercise has no other value, it will absolutely force you to concentrate on *what there is in Mr. Yates's paragraphs that has to be imitated.*

You have to imitate the number of sentences and their relative length and complexity, their grammatic structure.

You have to imitate detail that characterizes scene and actors.

You have to imitate the point of view.

You have to imitate the use of proper names and pronouns.

You have to imitate the emotional state of the characters that gives them their relationship in the scene.

In a word, you cannot do this sort of imitation without thinking pretty nimbly about what you are doing. You are performing one of the kinds of thought that is part of original composition, and if the example you are imitating serves as a kind of crutch, it also serves as a test of your power to shape the material of your own imagination to a predetermined form.

Even outright copying will force your mind down some of the grooves it has to follow when you do your own work. Try it and see. Copy out the last two pages of "The Yellow Raft." I think it is probably a good idea to do this work with the same tools you use in writing your own stories. That is, if you use a pen in your own work, use a pen now. If you use a typewriter or pencil, use a typewriter or pencil for copying. This may seem a ridiculously trivial instruction, bordering on superstition or magic rites. When I think about it rationally, it seems more than faintly ridiculous to me. But I know this, from my own experience and from the experience of many other serious and prolific writers: The writer's habits of thought have some strong, peculiar relation to the means he uses to get his words on paper. Some people cannot accommodate themselves to writing with a typewriter. Others feel stymied when they use pen or pencil. The main purpose of copying, I should think, is to permit you some sense that you are assuming the role of the original author. So eliminate any mechanical distraction that stands between you and the sense of how these words, sentences, and paragraphs must have flowed onto paper in the first place.

Copying obliges you to read all the words. So it may be an aid to bolstering up reading habits that are not good enough for a writer intent on learning his craft. It's amazing how often we read only enough of the words in each sentence to catch the general sense, only enough sentences in a paragraph to follow the general drift.

Another, somewhat looser, kind of imitation may be attractive to those who are most anxious about keeping their originality without stain. Both exercises I've just mentioned require an open book. But it's possible—and valuable sometimes—to imitate passages from someone else's work without constant checking for exactness. Here the values appear to be in the test put on one's memory for language of a special tone, for a way of composing sentences, and for combining sentences to form paragraphs. Such an exercise may sharpen one's sensitivity to style. Remember that not the least part of the memory on which a writer must rely is a memory of language and its resources in various combinations.

If I have begun by advocating some rather dry and mechanical forms of imitation, let me conclude by saying that imitation shades very gradually into all works that we properly think of as original. There cannot be, and probably there should never be, any piece of fiction that does not derive from other literary works, though the connections between one piece and whatever served as a model may be infinitely subtle and varied.

As a writer continues the practice of his art he will find more subtle and varied ways of drawing on what has already been done. Long after he stops getting any good from the simple kinds of imitation I have described, a writer may have evolved his own fashion of drawing on someone else's style or imagination. He may quite deliberately choose a theme or a mannerism that "belongs" to someone else with the intention of working his own variations on it. In such case he does not at all want to hide the source of his borrowing, but rather hopes it will be obvious to the reader.

In my own case I have found for some years that it helps me get started to work in the morning if I pull out a book and read a little bit—two or three paragraphs or a couple of stanzas of poetry. It doesn't matter, apparently, whether what I read has any overt connection with the thing I'm working on. All that matters is that what I read should be good enough to catch my own verbal imagination and drag it until it begins to move under its own power. Perhaps this reliance on an assist in taking off should not be categorized as imitation at all, and yet I have the idea that it may be at least an imitation of the creative drive my intuition finds in what I have read. And certainly it fulfills the one function that can be claimed for imitation —that of giving impetus and direction when the writer finds himself at a halt.

There is another practice that might be called either an exercise or a phase of composition—depending on what results are achieved by it. At any rate, it is experimental in nature and very often gives no rewards except a broader, clearer notion of the possibilities among which a writer may choose in presenting his story.

This might be given the general name *conversion*. It is vaguely comparable to transposing a piece of music from one key to another. If, for example, a story has been written in the first person ("I went home to Denmark after my father's death"), it can be a rewarding experiment to try the same story in the third person. ("After his father's death, Hamlet went home to Denmark.")

You might try such conversion on one of the stories in this book, but since it involves so much labor, you might well choose to try it instead on a story of your own, in the hope that a different manner of narration might give it a fresh start.

But before you begin your own revision, consider what changes would have to be made in some of these stories if the person of the narration were changed.

If you substituted the pronoun "I" for the name "Grace" in "The Best of Everything" the first several paragraphs might need no major alteration. It is perfectly plausible that someone might be reporting her own day at the office just before she is to be married in the same objective terms the author has used. But . . . when we come to the flashback describing the courtship that has preceded the present scene there would be a real necessity for the narrator to justify her choice of Ralph as a husband. The sleepwalking inertia that seems, in the present version, to be carrying her helplessly into this marriage would not

57

be acceptable at all if it were offered as explanation by a girl explaining her own case. (That's probably a sufficient reason, already, for leaving Yates's story as it is. We need go no further with our imaginary conversion than is required to show what alterations would have to be made if the manner of narration were changed.)

If "The Yellow Raft" were converted into a story told in the first person, again the changes in the early paragraphs would be minimal, merely the mechanical insertion of the first person pronoun, with appropriate grammatic adjustments. But, once the plane is in the water and the pilot has climbed onto the raft, a great deal more attention would be paid, more space given to his sufferings and hopes and recollections if the story were told by him. The conversion, that is, would require extensive adjustments of proportion.

And the use of a first person narration would mean the loss of the peculiar, haunting tone that makes the story so memorable. It is just the non-human objectivity of the event which serves so well to induce compassion in the present version.

The end (and several other parts) of "In the Zoo" would have to be recast if that story were converted from first person to third person narration. As it stands, the partly controlled hysteria of the narrator is presented as dramatically as it would be by an actress reading the part from the stage. ". . . I move across the car to watch the fields as they slip by. They are alfalfa fields, but you can bet your bottom dollar they are chockablock with marijuana." We do not have to be told that amusement mingles with self-disgust in the mind of the character, because in her own voice as narrator she expresses that mixture. But if we denied her her voice by changing the method of narration, either the hysteria would have to be named for what it is or an entirely different means of dramatizing it would have to be worked out.

With these hints from your reading in mind, do a full

job of converting one of your stories—one that doesn't quite satisfy you, of course. Experiments of this kind with technique can be the means of discovering a good story lurking half-hidden within an indifferent one.

Of course there are more ways of converting—or recasting—stories than by shifting the person of the narration.

For practice in revision you might try converting a grim and bleak story into comedy.

Try making fantasy from realism and realism from fantasy.

Try converting a story told mostly in author's prose into one made up mostly of dramatic dialogue.

Cut a story up into its separate paragraphs. (Yes, with scissors.) Make a new arrangement of paragraphs, write whatever connective passages are necessary to make the new arrangement coherent, and paste the result together to make a new manuscript. Does this strike you as being akin to cutting out paper dolls? It isn't, and even if it were it could help you convince yourself that a work of fiction is a plastic thing that *may* be rearranged into innumerable forms. When you realize that fully, you'll handle your own work with more freedom and authority. You'll stop being bossed by the qualities in it that are merely accidental.

Try reducing a story to half its length without losing essential meaning. In the same spirit, build one up by adding scenes where narrative passages served before.

Try replacing all proper nouns with pronouns in a story. This experiment will call for an adjustment of modifiers to keep identities separate and distinct. It is from the adjustments that you learn.

Enough. I have suggested exercises and experiments in revision that could keep anyone busy for a long time—

and keep him from doing the new stories he should be writing.

Remember that exercises and experiments are not ends in themselves. They are tonics, not bread. The writer—who must usually be his own doctor—has the responsibility of prescribing them for himself when he "can't get started" or when his technique proves insufficient for something he has begun.

It should go without saying that exercises ought to be undertaken with the same seriousness that goes into an original work. Unless you do your best, you might as well leave them alone.

And what if, in an exercise, you do better work than you have ever done before? I still say you ought to throw the result away—though there is no law against keeping it in your drawer or notebook for a while.

Only don't be afraid of losing something irreplaceable when you do discard well-done fragments. If you have unearthed some ideas, some phrases, or some scenes that are really your own and are deeply rooted in your emotions, you will lose nothing by dropping them out of sight.

Picasso said once, "When I paint a passage that is pretty, I rub it out, and after a while it comes back beautiful." That is the voice of a man who knows himself and knows how the creative process works through him. Remember this quotation. Trust your unconscious memory to retain what is important in your fragmentary successes.

And remember that however pretty they are, fragments have no real literary value until your imagination incorporates them into the unity of a complete story.

THE

STORIES

That Lovely Green Boat

This is an example of *first person narration* in which one of the main characters tells the story as he witnessed it and participated in it. Yet a great deal of the story is presented *objectively* and *dramatically*. Fortunately not every paragraph begins with the pronoun *I,* and the character of the narrator is revealed to us more by his dialogue and action than by any introspective examination of how he feels.

The boat mentioned in the title is obviously a *symbol*. It stands for something to the characters, and it stands for something (a little more subtle) to the reader.

The *setting* of the story—the river and the nearby house—plays a very important part.

The *understatement* (see Chap. 8) in both dialogue and narrator's prose is a tonal device for suggesting the strength of emotion spent on relatively unimportant acts.

The *climax* of the story occurs when Helen destroys the boat. What purpose is served by the episode with the bat in section V? Is it anti-climactic?

The story is realistic, but the *tone* of nostalgic lamentation for the delicate blunders of adolescence throws a faintly romantic haze over everything.

That Lovely Green Boat

by

WILLIAM BERGE

She was a duck boat, you know, like the kind you've seen and hungered after in the catalogues you look through during winter nights when the river's frozen hard and black like granite, and the wind is moaning to come in, and the train whistles are howling like souls come out of Chippahanock Cemetery. Only in the catalogue, her lightness and smoothness don't show, and you can't feel her turn in her own length or guess how fast she'll go upstream against an east wind and the waves chopping at her.

She was made of thin lath, her bow decked over, and she was painted light green—the color of maple leaves in early spring, and varnished with clear varnish and sanded and varnished and sanded again, and worked on with steel wool until the bottom was as smooth as the granite ice in winter that froze without wind. She was swift and light, like a kingfisher, and she seemed blonde in her greenness.

She would have been perfect for a light motor, if the

back end had been built up stronger, but we didn't have a motor. But she rowed well, and nothing could touch her. And she looked blonde in her greenness.

We would come down to her by the river early in the morning—the three of us, Carl, his sister Helen, and me—and she would be waiting for us there on the sand that had been left by the June rise of the river, and her greenness and the dry gold sand and Helen's hair all seemed blonde and light and lovely at once.

Helen and Carl and I would come down to the river early in the morning and find it smooth, without a ripple, save where a snag divided the surface or a whiff of wind ruffled it like a ribbon; and we would get in the boat and row out on the dark glass, heading downstream with the sun behind us, for the Mississippi flows from east to west there. We would anchor her on the sandbar that ran down the middle of the river, lining her bow on the trees that stood a breath above the far bend to make sure she was over the center, and then we could get out of the boat in water only up to our knees, and walking toward shore, steadily go deeper until the water was over our heads and as deep as anyone could want.

We wore suits that summer, though it was early in the morning, for Carl was sixteen, and I was fourteen, and Helen was just fourteen, and she didn't have just nipples any more like a boy, but soft round swellings the shape of lemons or young pears. And I wished I was her brother instead of Carl so that her Uncle John would be my uncle too, and then I could stay there on the river all year around, fishing and swimming and skating, and rowing her in the green duck boat.

THAT LOVELY GREEN BOAT

Then, while we were swimming, the river would begin to break up like a girl's skin that gets wet and cold
and then wrinkles, but you would never see it doing this,
but all at once you would look up and see that the mirror was shattered and shrivelled the way you find it at
noon or any other time of the day; and you would feel
just under your skin the peacefulness gone out of the
the river; and you would know the river's night was
over and that it was time for breakfast.

Aunt Jane Springer would have a pile of pancakes as
big as plates waiting for us, and after breakfast we
would run the trot lines and pull up the fish traps that
were longer than a man is tall, and the length of a man's
arm across, shaped in a cylinder of strong wire with an
entrance like a cone that a fish could come in by but
never leave again.

And then, if Carl didn't start working in the garage,
making something like bird houses or broom holders or
anything you could make in the winter when it was too
cold to go outside, or if he didn't have chores to do, the
three of us would cross to the island and hunt for coon
tracks, or stalk the big blue herons, or shoot crows or
swim off the bank. It was deep along the shore of the
island, so deep in places that you could not touch bottom when you dived—even by holding a rock in your
hands when you went down; and you would come up,
sometimes, with your chest feeling crushed and then
about to explode and then crushed again; and once my
nose bled and I could not go down again all day.

But sometimes, when Carl stayed behind, Helen and
I would cross the island and lie on the bank on the

WILLIAM BERGE

channel side and watch for the tow boats pushing their barges up or down the river, and if the *Mark Twain* or the *Lone Star* came along, we waved, because their crews always waved back. Sometimes we saw diesels, but we always felt sad about the diesels—both of us—because they were so small and blunt and ugly and work-a-day, and never so nice as the stern-wheelers.

At night, the three of us slept on the sleeping porch—Carl on my left and Helen on my right, if I was lying on my back. Carl always fell asleep immediately, like a stone dropping into the river, but Helen and I would light the lamp between our cots and read until midnight. Sometimes Carl was troubled and talked in his sleep, and once he got up and walked completely around his bed talking in his sleep, and then lay down again without waking up. Helen and I would ask him questions and he would answer the sound of our words but not the sense, saying, "Got to tie up the boat. That lovely green boat's going to float away. Got to tie up the boat."

Things would happen to me at night that summer, and in the morning I would wake and find them and think I had some awful disease until finally I was so worried about other people catching it from me that I told Carl about it, but he said it was regular and natural enough. And he took me out in the green duck boat and talked to me and connected it up with other things I already knew; and then he gave me makings and we smoked and just drifted.

Every day was maple-green and gold and lovely that summer.

THAT LOVELY GREEN BOAT

II

One day in August as Helen and I sat resting after a swim off the dock, the water drying on us leaving our skins wrinkled as though with age, one of those high-priced, syrup-colored, inboard motorboats came barrelling down the river, passed us, and then made a wide sweeping turn just inside the sandbar, and came back upstream.

"My, that's a fine boat," Helen said.

"Yes, it is," I said.

The motor cut out just then, and the boat coasted over before the dock like a fat mallard hen floating half asleep with the current, but coming upstream and being braked by the current so it could land with just a little bump at the far end of the dock. A brown-haired boy about as old as Carl held the boat to the dock and in a voice just a cut above normal talking said, "Do you want a ride?"

He said it in the way a man with five dollars offers to loan you a dollar just to show you he's got money and can afford to borrow out.

"No, thanks," I said. "We got boats of our own."

"I see you have," he said, as though I had been trying to explain to him an arithmetic problem he had solved the year before. "You got a motor for that green boat?"

"Don't want a motor," I said. "Rowing, she stays on the water. With a motor, she'd fly."

WILLIAM BERGE

"Do *you* want a ride?" he said again, nodding his head toward Helen.

"I told you once—"

"I don't mean you, I mean your sister."

"He's not my brother," Helen said. She didn't even look at me when she spoke.

"Do you want a ride?" the boy said again.

"No, she doesn't want a ride," I said.

"Yes, I'd like a ride," Helen said, as though she had just been awakened for breakfast.

"Wait a minute, Helen, you don't even know his—"

But she was running down the dock to stop suddenly by the boat and put her hand out, touching and petting the syrup-colored deck as though it was a horse's neck. "Yes, I'd like a ride," she said again, and she stepped down into the boat and settled on the leather seat like a great blue heron feeling for land under her when she's coming in to land big and awkward against a rough skipping wind.

The stranger gunned the motor and they cut away from the dock and up the river. I watched the boat go flying up the river and then go out of sight around the point. And I watched after it was gone until I couldn't hear the motor any more—as if I could watch instead of hear its sound—and I knew they must be up near Andalusia by then.

I sat on the dock and splashed my feet in the water and got cold and shivered and wrote my initials in the oil scum on the barrels that hold up the platform of the dock, and then wrote Helen's initials and then scratched them out and got up and ran and dived off the dock and hit the water wrong so that I was hurt where a boy

THAT LOVELY GREEN BOAT

hurts the worst and felt sick as though I had swallowed too much river water, and then came back to the dock swimming on my back, and crawled up on the platform and banged my shin and lay down on my back with my knees up, watching the sky and the trees change suddenly from blue and green-gold to red to hot white and then to October dun—all in a minute.

Helen was late for supper—so late Aunt Jane Springer got mad and told us to go ahead and eat without Helen, and asked herself out loud where Helen could have gone —clear up to the Rock Point dam, certainly not much farther. And then, as we were sitting down, we heard the motor faintly like a fly buzzing outside the screen door, and then it commenced to get louder and pretty soon it sounded like a nighthawk coming out of a dive, and we knew that the stranger had cut his motor and was coasting upstream to the dock. Then the motor gunned up again and in a few seconds it began to die away up the river. Helen came in then with her cheeks showing red even under her sunburn, and she was pretty and breathless and a little nervous and she asked Aunt Jane's pardon for being late. She would have been pretty any other day but this—her hair the color of dry gold sand and her skin blushing red under the color of wet gold sand—but I didn't even look at her.

But by bed-time, I could forgive her, and after we had undressed on the dark porch, standing with our backs to each other—Carl was already in bed—I said to her, "Do you want to read tonight?"

"Not especially," she said.

"You can read the book I got," I said.

WILLIAM BERGE

"I don't want to read it."

"I'm almost done with it, anyway," I said. "You can go ahead and read it."

"But I don't want to read it."

"Oh, go ahead," I said. "I can finish it after you're done."

"But I don't even want to start it," she said.

"All right then," I said.

"And please turn out the light," she said. "I can't sleep with the light in my eyes."

"All right," I said.

The next morning, Carl and I ran the trot lines by ourselves; Helen stayed on the dock. She hadn't even gone swimming with us before breakfast, but had slept right up until breakfast. I rowed while Carl caught the floats and ran us down along the lines rebaiting the empty hooks and taking off the fish we had caught. As we were running the third line, we heard the sound of a motor and we saw the stranger sweep around a half turn and coast up to the dock. Helen got in the boat, and they went ripping away.

"Handsome boat," Carl said.

"Yes, I guess it is," I said.

She hadn't even told us his name.

Carl and I went hunting for crows on the island with his twenty-two rifle, but we didn't get a thing except a rain crow I shot. The crows stayed on the island nights, and at dawn they flew eastward over the trees cawing a racket, and then turned south to the mainland to hunt

THAT LOVELY GREEN BOAT

out cornfields. Not getting any crows made Carl mad, and my shooting the rain crow made him madder.

"What did you shoot that for?" he said.

"It's a crow, isn't it?" I said.

"Heck, you know better than that. It's a yellow-billed cuckoo. What did you shoot it for?"

"It's a rain crow," I said again. I didn't know why I had shot it. We had just been walking along and when I heard it calling, in a tone like it was pleased with itself, "Tyok, tyok, tyok," I just up and banged away at it.

"It's a rain crow but it ain't a black crow. What's the matter—you color blind or something?"

We walked over to where it had fallen and we found it was still alive. The shot had gone through its chest without killing it. Its chest pumped up and down squirting out blood with each pump, and it didn't make a sound but looked up at me with the eye in the left side of its head. I wished it had died right away.

"Get a stick and kill it," Carl said.

"You kill it," I said.

"It's not my bird," he said. "You started the job, now finish it."

I turned and began to walk back toward the river, and Carl shouted after me, "I'll be damned if I'll finish it for you."

"Hold your horses," I said. "I'm just going to look for a rock."

"The heck you are." He knew there weren't any rocks on this side of the island where the banks are cut out so high above the river.

"The heck I'm not." I broke a stick from a dead

WILLIAM BERGE

branch and went back and stood over the bird and held my breath and counted three and smashed it. Carl had started toward the boat when I had gone back to the bird. I caught up with him at the boat.

"It's bad luck to kill a rain crow," he said quietly, as though telling me a secret I hadn't heard.

"You got holes in your head," I said.

"What you so mad about?"

"I'm not mad!"

"If you weren't mad, you wouldn't shout so telling me you weren't."

"Oh, go to." I untied the line and threw it over the bow of the boat.

"You shot your luck," Carl said. "Going to rain like hell."

"Go to hell."

"Like a cow pissing off a flat rock," Carl said. He took out his makings and gave me a paper and passed me the sack of tobacco. "Trouble is, I'll be in the same rain you are."

I rolled the tobacco in the paper, wet the edge, and wiped it down. Carl struck a wooden match and held it toward me. I puffed on the cigarette. "Do you want to row or should I?"

"You can row," Carl said.

At supper, all Helen could talk about was Richard Wellman and his motorboat and her rides with him up and down the river. She was just brimming full of Richard Wellman, like low cut banks in a spring rise. His grandfather had been a contractor; no, he had not lost anything in the depression; yes, he was in love with

THAT LOVELY GREEN BOAT

his grandson; certainly, he was going to send Richard to college; sure, he was the one who bought Richard the boat; also, he had set up Richard's father in business; oh, it was a wonderful summer camp he was building above Andalusia—it even had an electric pump so they could have a toilet in the house. She just splashed and flooded and ripped with Richard Wellman.

I excused myself early and went down to the dock and got the double-ended Mississippi fish boat and rowed over to the island. The sun was just going down and the horizon was all fire half way up the sky so I knew it wouldn't rain the next day. But I went back into the woods and found the rain crow and buried it anyway.

By the time I got back to the boat, the river was dark and there were no lights on shore yet. I rowed for where I thought the dock should be, and when I came close to shore, I heard Carl's voice—not shouting, but talking low as though speaking to a man next to him—"Pull on your right oar a wee bit. There's a little less current to-night. Steady. That's it."

It was an awful quiet night and his voice carried as over a telephone wire. He took the bow line and tied it to a ring.

"Did you bury it?"

"Yes," I said.

"That was a good idea."

"Sky was red tonight."

"I know," he said. "Maybe burying it will keep the rain away."

"I hope so."

We went behind the garage and Carl gave me makings and we rolled cigarettes and had a long smoke.

"I think I know why you're mad," he said.

"I'm not mad," I said, this time quietly.

"Well, then, I know why you would be if you were mad," he said.

"Does it show?" I said.

"Not much," he said. "Not so's you'd notice it."

"I buried it," I said.

"Yes, you did."

"I killed it and buried it."

"I know you did."

The cigarette was sending me off the ground and then bringing me back and then sending me off again. I was inhaling.

"But don't worry," he said. "Have you noticed the river?"

"What about it?"

"Have you noticed it?" he said.

"Not especially," I said.

"Look at that maple sapling standing in the water. See the marks?"

"She's dropping, that's all."

"Yes, she's dropping, and that's enough."

He handed me more makings, and just then it came to me and I laughed so hard I blew the tobacco off the paper. The river was down six inches at the very least.

III

The next morning, Richard Wellman came down the river and offered us rides on his surf board. He had it

Writing Fiction

strapped on the deck, of all places. He didn't give a
tinker's dam about the finish.

Carl told him not to go below the dock, and he asked
why, but Carl just said not to go below the dock or
nobody there would ride. Richard said he wouldn't, so
we all took rides, but Helen took the most of all. She
hated to give up the board, and anybody with half an
eye could see Richard had just made the offer to Carl
and me to be polite. He and Helen took turns riding the
board and steering the boat.

When Helen rode the board, she screamed and yelled
all the time she was whipping back and forth behind the
boat; and sometimes she would stand on one leg and
hold on with one arm, or else she would try other
tricks you might see in the movies and she would get
flipped off. But she always came back for more. She
was as golden brown and wild as a hawk.

After dinner, Richard came back towing one of those
tin, non-sinkable rowboats behind him. He told us what
we already knew—that it had air-tight compartments
and so on, and then he asked us to race. We lined up his
boat and our two and I said he could have first choice,
but Helen jumped up—

"I want the duck boat. I want to race too, and I want
the duck boat."

"Sure," Richard said. "Then I'll take my own boat."

You could tell he had not been on the river much
because he preferred every kind of boat to the double-
ended fishing boat, and plainly, he did not know how
well balanced they were for all their size, nor how light
and swift they were for all their clumsy looks, nor how
little water they drew for all their depth of side, nor

WILLIAM BERGE

even how practical they were for running trot lines or setting nets or fish traps. He preferred the tin boats because their lines were more nearly like those of his motorboat, but they were not easy rowing; and his only right choice had been when he preferred the duck boat to the double-ender. And then his choice had come from its having lines like those of a speed boat.

We were to row up to the point and back, Carl giving the word go, and deciding the winner. When Carl said go, I started out slow and watched Richard over my shoulder. He was rowing fast and had got a good lead from the start, but his tin boat was awkward and he was rowing with his arms instead of his back. Being half a head taller than me wouldn't help him if he did that, so I set my back into it with long easy pulls.

Helen was leading in the duck boat, and I could tell he was letting her lead because he was sure I had the wrong boat to win by, and that he could keep ahead of me and still let her win. I was just behind him when he turned at the point. Helen was already started downstream, and she was laughing so hard she could barely row. She couldn't see how Richard was sweating at the turn nor how he chopped with his right oar, turning toward the bank.

I turned out into the stream, and current out from the point helped swing my bow around and I started down even with Richard. He saw I was getting more current than he was, and he tried to correct it but it was no use. I was using my back and he was using his arms.

Half way to the dock, I caught up with Helen, and then thinking of how much she liked to win, I dropped in just behind her. She wasn't laughing any more, but

THAT LOVELY GREEN BOAT

rowing hard. She reached the dock half a length ahead
of me, and then we just sat there waiting for Richard.

"It was a good race," I said.

"Uh-huh."

"But he doesn't know his boats."

"He's got a motorboat," she said.

"But I beat him rowing."

"I've got eyes," she said.

"Did you want him to win?"

"It was a race. I wanted to win."

"Well, you won."

"I suppose you let me win," she said, mocking me
with the tone of her voice. She looked at me for a
minute with her mouth open. "Darn you. Darn you if
you did."

Richard stayed to supper and met Aunt Jane and
Uncle John Springer. He even started calling them Aunt
Jane and Uncle John right away, and nobody seemed to
mind. I felt uncomfortable enough to be sitting on tacks,
and I was glad when Carl said that one of the trot lines
was gone and that he and I should go look for it.

"Either she's loose or the float got busted and sank."

"If it's loose, it should be snagged somewhere downstream," I said. For floats, we used gallon glass jugs,
and if one of them broke, there was usually no finding
the line.

"Well, let's commence to begin to start," he said. "I'll
take the fish boat and look over toward the island."

"I doubt that it would have gotten over there," I said.

"There was a south wind today," he said.

"But it wouldn't blow far dragging line."

WILLIAM BERGE

"It might have snagged on the bar," he said. "The river's awful low on the bar."

We worked our way down the river slowly, searching the low places, Carl over by the bar and I over by the shore. We had been out about half an hour when Helen and Richard went spinning by us in his tin boat. They hailed us, and we hailed back, but I didn't pay any more attention to them, although I did notice they landed quite a ways down and went in among the maples.

But I was really surprised when a while later I looked up once and saw their boat just ahead of me. I tied on to her and took out the makings Carl had given me and had a smoke. I looked over to where Carl was working along the bar, and he waved his arm and started rowing back upstream. "It must have busted and sank," he said just loud enough to hear. "Going back up?"

"In a minute," I said, and I blew a puff of smoke for him to see.

"O-kay," he said. "I'll see you."

Just as I flipped the butt into the river, Helen came out of the maple grove walking fast, her head down. She didn't see me until she got right up to their boat, and then she sort of jumped and said, "Oh." She looked back once at the maple grove, and then she said, "Just what do you think you're doing here?" Her face was red under the sun tan.

"I just stopped for a smoke."

"Oh? Where's your cigarette?"

"I just now flipped it away."

"Yes you did."

"I can't show you the butt, but I can let you see the makings if you want to."

THAT LOVELY GREEN BOAT

"You haven't got them. You're just spying around."

"Here they are."

"Well, why don't you roll me one?"

"You're awful jumpy tonight."

"Am I? I hadn't noticed."

"What's the matter?" I said.

"Nothing. Nothing's the matter."

"Where's Richard?"

"Back there," she said, waving her cigarette at the maple grove.

"Did he do anything to you?"

"Who, Richard? No, of course not."

"Well, if he did—"

"But he didn't," she said.

"You kind of like him, don't you?"

"What if I did?"

"Do you like him enough— Never mind. Here's a light. Catch it."

"What were you saying?" she said.

"Me? Oh, nothing. Do you want to ride up with me?"

"I'm waiting for Richard."

"But I can take you up as well as not."

"No," she said, "I'm waiting for Richard."

"All right." I threw her the sack of makings. "Cast me off and I'll get out of here."

She untied my line and threw it over the bow.

"See you at the house," I said.

"Rob—"

"Yes?" She hadn't called me Rob in a long time.

"Rob—you won't say anything. About this?"

"About what? About something I never saw? You got holes in your head."

WILLIAM BERGE

As I rowed home, my back pointed upstream, I saw the sun hover on the horizon like a hawk just before it drops. The sun was just one great big red ball, but there was no redness outside of it; the sky was white all around it. Then it dropped slowly, keeping its color all inside itself, leaving the sky white around it—but not with the white of clouds.

When I reached the landing, Carl was waiting for me.

"You took a long time," he said. "What were you doing?"

"Just looking."

"See anything?"

"The sun. Just the sun, that's all," I said. "Did you see it?"

"Yes."

"Maybe not for two days," I said.

"Maybe not. Maybe not tomorrow, maybe not even the day after," he said. "But then—like a cow off a flat rock."

"Burying doesn't do any good, I guess."

"No," he said, "I guess it doesn't."

IV

A west wind came up and wakened me about midnight. It howled up the river, and then slowly began to swing up from the south, and then shifted back again, trying to collect every cloud in five states. It would be angling across the river by morning probably, and settling down for a good blow.

Helen woke up and asked what was all the noise, and

THAT LOVELY GREEN BOAT

when I said that it was the wind, she just rolled over muttering, "Awful lot of racket."

Even Carl was troubled in his sleep, and once or twice he said, "Got to tie up the boat. That lovely green boat's going to float away. Got to tie up the boat."

Richard came bouncing down the river late in the afternoon as the three of us were standing on the dock looking at the river. Carl and I had gone out in the morning and had taken in the trot lines and had pulled both boats up on shore, and we were surprised to see Richard out, though it looked like a lot of fun bouncing over the waves like that.

"You better get your boat out of the water," I said as he tied up at the dock. He had been able to land downstream because the wind was so strong.

"It's a lot more fun like this," he said.

"So is jumping off a moving train," Carl said.

"Is everything all right?" Richard said to Helen.

"Sure," she said. "Why not?"

"Good. I came down to see—just to make sure. And to take you for a ride."

"She doesn't want to go for a ride in this," I said.

"Yes, I do," Helen said.

"You've got holes in your head if you go out in this." It was growing as dark as evening; I couldn't even see the trees on which we lined up the bar.

"But you like to go out in storms yourself," she said. "Remember when Mr. McCormick let you and Carl sail his boat last summer and then took it away from you because you always sailed at night or out in a storm? Well, I like it too."

WILLIAM BERGE

"But not today," I said. "And you're not going out either—is she, Carl?"

"You listen to what he says," Carl said.

"Don't call Carl into this," she said, and she climbed down into the boat. "Hurry up and cast off, Richard." Richard gunned the motor and the boat slid away from the dock and began to pick up speed. "You're just jealous, that's all," she shouted back to us. Big drops of rain began to fall then, but we could hear her laughter even above their splash.

"Look out for the bar!" I shouted. "Stay away from the sandbar! The river's low!" But they were too far away now to hear me above the wind and the rain.

"Don't worry," Carl said, "she can line the bar."

"Oh yeah! Look!" I pointed downstream to where the darkness had hidden the trees at the bend.

"Damn! Goddamn! And all the water's rough water now. Nobody can see a bar by ripples or drift now."

The rain began to come down heavy—like a cow off a flat rock—and Helen and Richard swung downstream hugging the island bank. If praying could raise water, the river would have come up a foot just then.

"They're all right if they keep close to the island for the length of the bar," Carl said.

As they passed us on the far side of the river, I shouted again, "Stay clear of the bar!"

As though to hear me better, Helen stood up in the boat holding on to the windshield, and just then Richard whipped the boat toward the center of the river, smacking the white-capped waves, and flipped Helen out. Helen had barely hit the water when the boat struck the bar and ripped out her bottom with a sound like

THAT LOVELY GREEN BOAT

more thunder. Carl and I were already running to the fish boat.

I got in and set the oars while he untied her and shoved her out. I pulled straight for Helen, thinking the wind would offset the current, but there was more wind than I had expected and Carl had to correct me: "Left oar, left oar."

I braced my feet and stiffened my legs, reaching and pulling with my back. As we came near Helen, Carl shouted, "Swing her, swing her," and I pushed the right against pulling the left, the boat shivered and paused for an instant, and Carl reached out and dragged Helen into the boat.

"Go for Richard," he said while Helen's legs were still in the water. Helen choked and spat the water out of her throat.

"Richard?" she said.

"We're coming to him," Carl said.

I was too winded to talk. I glanced over my shoulder once to locate the motorboat. It was beginning to settle and I couldn't see why until I thought that the speed of the boat must have carried it past the bar and into deeper water, or else the waves had knocked it off—or maybe both.

My right oar struck the bar and Carl jumped out. The water was only at his waist when he reached the motorboat, but Richard—knocked out against the wheel —was already settling up to his neck. The bow of the boat was sinking first, the stern still caught on a high place on the bar. Carl lifted Richard out of the motorboat, floated him to the bow of the rowboat, and then, ducking under him, lifted him into the rowboat.

WILLIAM BERGE

"Get in the stern," Carl said to Helen. "We want some weight in back. Slide over, Rob."

We each took an oar and pulled for shore, Carl counting, "One . . . two . . . three . . . One . . ."

As the boat struck beach, Carl and I grabbed Richard and ran for the house. Uncle John came down the yard to help us. Aunt Jane swung the door open.

"I've already called the doctor," she said. She swung the door closed, turned toward the cot where Richard now lay, then swung around again. "What in heaven's name is Helen doing?"

I looked toward the river. Helen, in the green duck boat, was pulling for the wreck. She was already almost half way there.

"She's going to haul in the wreck," I said. "She'll pull the back end out of that boat."

I didn't stop for Carl but ran out the door and down to the double-ender. Helen had reached the wreck by the time I was launched, but I knew it would take her some time to tie on to it. I looked around once to set my course, and then didn't look again, but pulled and pulled and pulled. Then I heard the crack of parting wood and I turned just in time to see the duck boat shoot suddenly forward, Helen's legs kicking up in the air, and then begin to settle stern first. When I reached her, she was standing on the bar.

"You goddamned fool," I said.

I took both oars from the duck boat and jammed their handles first into a high part of the bar and tied the motorboat and the duck boat to them. The oar blades were chipped and broken. She must have set both blades into the sandbar to use the oars as levers.

THAT LOVELY GREEN BOAT

"If they stay, they stay," I said. "If they don't, they don't. Now get in."

On the island, a tree fell with rush of breaking limbs ending in a sudden boom. I was too tired to row fast, but I used the wind as much as I could, and we went at a pretty good clip. At the shore, we dragged the boat up on the bank and went up to the house. The doctor's Ford V-8 stood in the driveway.

"Everything will be all right," he was saying as we opened the screen door.

v

Helen and I both woke to the sound of wings beating against the screens. It was earlier than we usually got up, but Carl was already gone. We looked around the porch to locate the sound. The sky was not even gray yet; light kind of oozed through the clouds, seeming like wet and pulpy rotten wood.

The wings fluttered again and I looked up to the ceiling. Two bats, one inside the porch and one outside, kept flying toward each other, hitting the screen, and then flying off. It was as though they were trying to kiss through the screen.

"I thought bats never hit things," I said.

"Try and catch it," Helen said.

The bat inside the porch wacked against the screen and glided off onto Helen's bed. I jerked the blanket over it and then reached under and caught it with my hand.

"Put it outside," Helen said.

WILLIAM BERGE

"Oh, no. Bats are lovely birds. Feel how soft she is."

"Keep it away. I don't want it in my hair."

"It won't get in your hair if I hold it. Here, touch it."

She reached out one finger in a scared way as though hunting for a set mouse-trap in the dark. Then, when she touched it and felt how soft and silky was its fur, she petted it with her whole hand.

"It is lovely," she said. "But bats aren't birds. They're mammals the same as people."

"We ought to keep him," I said. "Or her, whichever it is."

"What would you feed him?" Helen said.

"I don't know, but we could find out."

"No, you better let him go."

"Why? Wouldn't you like to be able to take her out of her cage and pet her every so often? You just said she was lovely."

"No, it would die," she said.

"Do you think it would?"

"I'm sure of it. All wild things are like that. Remember that little rabbit Carl caught in his box trap last summer? We fed it everything but it wouldn't eat, and it died."

" 'Coons don't."

"But you have to keep them chained," she said. "And once they get loose, they go hiking off to the nearest river or woods."

"Yes, I guess they do."

"Wait till I get dressed and we'll put it outside."

I put the bat under a blanket and tucked the blanket edges under the mattress, and then I began to dress.

THAT LOVELY GREEN BOAT

I was watching Helen dress, and she watched me, and neither of us said a thing. Her breasts were shaped more like lemons than young pears. They looked soft and tender and shy like wild flowers that die quickly when you close them in your hand. But I wanted to touch them just as you always want to pick the flowers.

When we had finished dressing, we both smiled, and I felt my face go red as I saw hers go red.

"Let's put the bat out," she said.

I took the bat from under the blanket and we went outside. Neither one of us wanted to let it go. Helen kept stroking it. Its fur was lovely, soft, and dark.

Carl came toward us from the dock. "What you got there?"

"A bat," Helen said. "It was on the porch."

"So that's what it was. I got up before light this morning, and when I opened the door, I knew something came in. It brushed my shoulder, but I thought it was a bird."

"Isn't he lovely?" Helen said.

"What are you going to do with her?" Carl said.

"Let him go," Helen said.

"When?"

"Right now," I said. "I'm going to let her go right now." I threw the bat into the air. It flew around crazily for a minute, and then winged away toward the trees by the river. We watched it until it disappeared, and still we looked after it. The second bat came from around the house and shuttled back and forth, but going always toward the river and the trees. Then it too disappeared.

Finally, Helen turned and said, "The boats?"

WILLIAM BERGE

"The motorboat's there," Carl said, "but it isn't worth a tinker's dam now."

"And the duck boat?" I asked, though somehow I had already guessed what he would say.

"Gone," he said. "That lovely green boat has floated away."

The Lady with the Pet Dog

Third person narration. The story is realistic, but the presentation is not particularly *objective.* Here we find the *omniscient author* expounding the details and the generalities of Gurov's thought, character, and milieu. The story is told from Gurov's *point of view,* but the author does not limit himself to Gurov's thought or experiences.

The *plot* is submerged. It may seem to you that there is no plot, but if you pay attention to the phases through which Gurov passes you will see its firm structure under the fluid surface.

The *settings* are used to hint the changes of mood and circumstance through which Gurov passes.

The ironic, melancholy *tone* rises chiefly, perhaps, from the surprises of the plot, but is enhanced by some of the rueful observations contributed by the author.

Note that this is the only story in this book which was not originally written in English, and the only one written before 1940. Be on guard, a little, against picking up usages from this story that may be accidents of translation or somewhat outmoded fashions of narration.

The Lady with the Pet Dog

by

ANTON CHEKHOV

A new person, it was said, had appeared on the esplanade: a lady with a pet dog. Dmitry Dmitrich Gurov, who had spent a fortnight at Yalta and had got used to the place, had also begun to take an interest in new arrivals. As he sat in Vernet's confectionery shop, he saw, walking on the esplanade, a fair-haired young woman of medium height, wearing a beret; a white Pomeranian was trotting behind her.

And afterwards he met her in the public garden and in the square several times a day. She walked alone, always wearing the same beret and always with the white dog; no one knew who she was and everyone called her simply "the lady with the pet dog."

"If she is here alone without husband or friends," Gurov reflected, "it wouldn't be a bad thing to make her acquaintance."

He was under forty, but he already had a daughter twelve years old, and two sons at school. They had found a wife for him when he was very young, a stu-

ANTON CHEKHOV

dent in his second year, and by now she seemed half as old again as he. She was a tall, erect woman with dark eyebrows, stately and dignified and, as she said of herself, intellectual. She read a great deal, used simplified spelling in her letters, called her husband, not Dmitry, but Dimitry, while he privately considered her of limited intelligence, narrow-minded, dowdy, was afraid of her, and did not like to be at home. He had begun being unfaithful to her long ago——had been unfaithful to her often and, probably for that reason, almost always spoke ill of women, and when they were talked of in his presence used to call them "the inferior race."

It seemed to him that he had been sufficiently tutored by bitter experience to call them what he pleased, and yet he could not have lived without "the inferior race" for two days together. In the company of men he was bored and ill at ease, he was chilly and uncommunicative with them; but when he was among women he felt free, and knew what to speak to them about and how to comport himself; and even to be silent with them was no strain on him. In his appearance, in his character, in his whole make-up there was something attractive and elusive that disposed women in his favor and allured them. He knew that, and some force seemed to draw him to them, too.

Oft-repeated and really bitter experience had taught him long ago that with decent people——particularly Moscow people——who are irresolute and slow to move, every affair which at first seems a light and charming adventure inevitably grows into a whole problem of extreme complexity, and in the end a painful situation

THE LADY WITH THE PET DOG

is created. But at every new meeting with an interesting woman this lesson of experience seemed to slip from his memory, and he was eager for life, and everything seemed so simple and diverting.

One evening while he was dining in the public garden the lady in the beret walked up without haste to take the next table. Her expression, her gait, her dress, and the way she did her hair told him that she belonged to the upper class, that she was married, that she was in Yalta for the first time and alone, and that she was bored there. The stories told of the immorality in Yalta are to a great extent untrue; he despised them, and knew that such stories were made up for the most part by persons who would have been glad to sin themselves if they had had the chance; but when the lady sat down at the next table three paces from him, he recalled these stories of easy conquests, of trips to the mountains, and the tempting thought of a swift, fleeting liaison, a romance with an unknown woman of whose very name he was ignorant suddenly took hold of him.

He beckoned invitingly to the Pomeranian, and when the dog approached him, shook his finger at it. The Pomeranian growled; Gurov threatened it again.

The lady glanced at him and at once dropped her eyes.

"He doesn't bite," she said and blushed.

"May I give him a bone?" he asked; and when she nodded he inquired affably, "Have you been in Yalta long?"

"About five days."

"And I am dragging out the second week here."

There was a short silence.

ANTON CHEKHOV

"Time passes quickly, and yet it is so dull here!" she said, not looking at him.

"It's only the fashion to say it's dull here. A provincial will live in Belyov or Zhizdra and not be bored, but when he comes here it's 'Oh, the dullness! Oh, the dust!' One would think he came from Granada."

She laughed. Then both continued eating in silence, like strangers, but after dinner they walked together and there sprang up between them the light banter of people who are free and contented, to whom it does not matter where they go or what they talk about. They walked and talked of the strange light on the sea: the water was a soft, warm, lilac color, and there was a golden band of moonlight upon it. They talked of how sultry it was after a hot day. Gurov told her that he was a native of Moscow, that he had studied languages and literature at the university, but had a post in a bank; that at one time he had trained to become an opera singer but had given it up, that he owned two houses in Moscow. And he learned from her that she had grown up in Petersburg, but had lived in S— since her marriage two years previously, that she was going to stay in Yalta for about another month, and that her husband, who needed a rest, too, might perhaps come to fetch her. She was not certain whether her husband was a member of a Government Board or served on a Zemstvo Council, and this amused her. And Gurov learned too that her name was Anna Sergeyevna.

Afterwards in his room at the hotel he thought about her—and was certain that he would meet her the next day. It was bound to happen. Getting into bed he recalled that she had been a schoolgirl only recently, do-

THE LADY WITH THE PET DOG

ing lessons like his own daughter; he thought how much timidity and angularity there was still in her laugh and her manner of talking with a stranger. It must have been the first time in her life that she was alone in a setting in which she was followed, looked at, and spoken to for one secret purpose alone, which she could hardly fail to guess. He thought of her slim, delicate throat, her lovely gray eyes.

"There's something pathetic about her, though," he thought, and dropped off.

II

A week had passed since they had struck up an acquaintance. It was a holiday. It was close indoors, while in the street the wind whirled the dust about and blew people's hats off. One was thirsty all day, and Gurov often went into the restaurant and offered Anna Sergeyevna a soft drink or ice cream. One did not know what to do with oneself.

In the evening when the wind had abated they went out on the pier to watch the steamer come in. There were a great many people walking about the dock; they had come to welcome someone and they were carrying bunches of flowers. And two peculiarities of a festive Yalta crowd stood out: the elderly ladies were dressed like young ones and there were many generals.

Owing to the choppy sea, the steamer arrived late, after sunset, and it was a long time tacking about before it put in at the pier. Anna Sergeyevna peered at the steamer and the passengers through her lorgnette as though looking for acquaintances, and whenever she turned to Gurov her eyes were shining. She talked a great deal and asked questions jerkily, forgetting the next moment what she had asked; then she lost her lorgnette in the crush.

The festive crowd began to disperse; it was now too dark to see people's faces; there was no wind any more, but Gurov and Anna Sergeyevna still stood as though waiting to see someone else come off the steamer. Anna Sergeyevna was silent now, and sniffed her flowers without looking at Gurov.

"The weather has improved this evening," he said. "Where shall we go now? Shall we drive somewhere?"

She did not reply.

Then he looked at her intently, and suddenly embraced her and kissed her on the lips, and the moist fragrance of her flowers enveloped him; and at once he looked round him anxiously, wondering if anyone had seen them.

"Let us go to your place," he said softly. And they walked off together rapidly.

The air in her room was close and there was the smell of the perfume she had bought at the Japanese shop. Looking at her, Gurov thought: "What encounters life offers!" From the past he preserved the memory of carefree, good-natured women whom love made gay and who were grateful to him for the happiness he gave them, however brief it might be; and of women like his wife who loved without sincerity, with too many words, affectedly, hysterically, with an expression that it was not love or passion that engaged them but something more significant; and of two or three others, very beau-

THE LADY WITH THE PET DOG

tiful, frigid women, across whose faces would suddenly flit a rapacious expression—an obstinate desire to take from life more than it could give, and these were women no longer young, capricious, unreflecting, domineering, unintelligent, and when Gurov grew cold to them their beauty aroused his hatred, and the lace on their lingerie seemed to him to resemble scales.

But here there was the timidity, the angularity of inexperienced youth, a feeling of awkwardness; and there was a sense of embarrassment, as though someone had suddenly knocked at the door. Anna Sergeyevna, "the lady with the pet dog," treated what had happened in a peculiar way, very seriously, as though it were her fall—so it seemed, and this was odd and inappropriate. Her features drooped and faded, and her long hair hung down sadly on either side of her face; she grew pensive and her dejected pose was that of a Magdalene in a picture by an old master.

"It's not right," she said. "You don't respect me now, you first of all."

There was a watermelon on the table. Gurov cut himself a slice and began eating it without haste. They were silent for at least half an hour.

There was something touching about Anna Sergeyevna; she had the purity of a well-bred, naive woman who has seen little of life. The single candle burning on the table barely illumined her face, yet it was clear that she was unhappy.

"Why should I stop respecting you, darling?" asked Gurov. "You don't know what you're saying."

"God forgive me," she said, and her eyes filled with tears. "It's terrible."

ANTON CHEKHOV

"It's as though you were trying to exonerate yourself."

"How can I exonerate myself? No. I am a bad, low woman; I despise myself and I have no thought of exonerating myself. It's not my husband but myself I have deceived. And not only just now; I have been deceiving myself for a long time. My husband may be a good, honest man, but he is a flunkey! I don't know what he does, what his work is, but I know he is a flunkey! I was twenty when I married him. I was tormented by curiosity; I wanted something better. 'There must be a different sort of life,' I said to myself. I wanted to live! To live, to live! Curiosity kept eating at me—you don't understand it, but I swear to God I could no longer control myself; something was going on in me; I could not be held back. I told my husband I was ill, and came here. And here I have been walking about as though in a daze, as though I were mad; and now I have become a vulgar, vile woman whom anyone may despise."

Gurov was already bored with her; he was irritated by her naive tone, by her repentance, so unexpected and so out of place, but for the tears in her eyes he might have thought she was joking or play-acting.

"I don't understand, my dear," he said softly. "What do you want?"

She hid her face on his breast and pressed close to him.

"Believe me, believe me, I beg you," she said, "I love honesty and purity, and sin is loathsome to me; I don't know what I'm doing. Simple people say, 'The Evil One

THE LADY WITH THE PET DOG

has led me astray.' And I may say of myself now that the Evil One has led me astray."

"Quiet, quiet," he murmured.

He looked into her fixed, frightened eyes, kissed her, spoke to her softly and affectionately, and by degrees she calmed down, and her gaiety returned; both began laughing.

Afterwards when they went out there was not a soul on the esplanade. The town with its cypresses looked quite dead, but the sea was still sounding as it broke upon the beach; a single launch was rocking on the waves and on it a lantern was blinking sleepily.

They found a cab and drove to Oreanda.

"I found out your surname in the hall just now: it was written on the board—von Dideritz," said Gurov. "Is your husband German?"

"No; I believe his grandfather was German, but he is Greek Orthodox himself."

At Oreanda they sat on a bench not far from the church, looked down at the sea, and were silent. Yalta was barely visible through the morning mist; white clouds rested motionlessly on the mountaintops. The leaves did not stir on the trees, cicadas twanged, and the monotonous muffled sound of the sea that rose from below spoke of the peace, the eternal sleep awaiting us. So it rumbled below when there was no Yalta, no Oreanda here; so it rumbles now, and it will rumble as indifferently and as hollowly when we are no more. And in this constancy, in this complete indifference to the life and death of each of us, there lies, perhaps, a pledge of our eternal salvation, of the unceasing advance of life upon earth, of unceasing movement towards perfection. Sitting beside a young woman who in the dawn seemed so lovely, Gurov, soothed and spellbound by these magical surroundings—the sea, the mountains, the clouds, the wide sky—thought how everything is really beautiful in this world when one reflects: everything except what we think or do ourselves when we forget the higher aims of life and our own human dignity.

A man strolled up to them—probably a guard—looked at them and walked away. And this detail, too, seemed so mysterious and beautiful. They saw a steamer arrive from Feodosia, its lights extinguished in the glow of dawn.

"There is dew on the grass," said Anna Sergeyevna, after a silence.

"Yes, it's time to go home."

They returned to the city.

Then they met every day at twelve o'clock on the esplanade, lunched and dined together, took walks, admired the sea. She complained that she slept badly, that she had palpitations, asked the same questions, troubled now by jealousy and now by the fear that he did not respect her sufficiently. And often in the square or the public garden, when there was no one near them, he suddenly drew her to him and kissed her passionately. Complete idleness, these kisses in broad daylight exchanged furtively in dread of someone's seeing them, the heat, the smell of the sea, and the continual flitting before his eyes of idle, well-dressed, well-fed people, worked a complete change in him; he kept telling Anna Sergeyevna how beautiful she was, how seductive, was urgently passionate; he would not move a step away

THE LADY WITH THE PET DOG

from her, while she was often pensive and continually pressed him to confess that he did not respect her, did not love her in the least, and saw in her nothing but a common woman. Almost every evening rather late they drove somewhere out of town, to Oreanda or to the waterfall; and the excursion was always a success, the scenery invariably impressed them as beautiful and magnificent.

They were expecting her husband, but a letter came from him saying that he had eye-trouble, and begging his wife to return home as soon as possible. Anna Sergeyevna made haste to go.

"It's a good thing I am leaving," she said to Gurov. "It's the hand of Fate!"

She took a carriage to the railway station, and he went with her. They were driving the whole day. When she had taken her place in the express, and when the second bell had rung, she said, "Let me look at you once more—let me look at you again. Like this."

She was not crying but was so sad that she seemed ill and her face was quivering.

"I shall be thinking of you—remembering you," she said. "God bless you; be happy. Don't remember evil against me. We are parting forever—it has to be, for we ought never to have met. Well, God bless you."

The train moved off rapidly, its lights soon vanished, and a minute later there was no sound of it, as though everything had conspired to end as quickly as possible that sweet trance, that madness. Left alone on the platform, and gazing into the dark distance, Gurov listened to the twang of the grasshoppers and the hum of the telegraph wires, feeling as though he had just waked

ANTON CHEKHOV

up. And he reflected, musing, that there had now been another episode or adventure in his life, and it, too, was at an end, and nothing was left of it but a memory. He was moved, sad, and slightly remorseful: this young woman whom he would never meet again had not been happy with him; he had been warm and affectionate with her, but yet in his manner, his tone, and his caresses there had been a shade of light irony, the slightly coarse arrogance of a happy male who was, besides, almost twice her age. She had constantly called him kind, exceptional, high-minded; obviously he had seemed to her different from what he really was, so he had involuntarily deceived her.

Here at the station there was already a scent of autumn in the air; it was a chilly evening.

"It is time for me to go north, too," thought Gurov as he left the platform. "High time!"

III

At home in Moscow the winter routine was already established; the stoves were heated, and in the morning it was still dark when the children were having breakfast and getting ready for school, and the nurse would light the lamp for a short time. There were frosts already. When the first snow falls, on the first day the sleighs are out, it is pleasant to see the white earth, the white roofs; one draws easy, delicious breaths, and the season brings back the days of one's youth. The old limes and birches, white with hoar-frost, have a good-natured look; they are closer to one's heart than cy-

THE LADY WITH THE PET DOG

presses and palms, and near them one no longer wants to think of mountains and the sea.

Gurov, a native of Moscow, arrived there on a fine frosty day, and when he put on his fur coat and warm gloves and took a walk along Petrovka, and when on Saturday night he heard the bells ringing, his recent trip and the places he had visited lost all charm for him. Little by little he became immersed in Moscow life, greedily read three newspapers a day, and declared that he did not read the Moscow papers on principle. He already felt a longing for restaurants, clubs, formal dinners, anniversary celebrations, and it flattered him to entertain distinguished lawyers and actors, and to play cards with a professor at the physicians' club. He could eat a whole portion of meat stewed with pickled cabbage and served in a pan, Moscow style.

A month or so would pass and the image of Anna Sergeyevna, it seemed to him, would become misty in his memory, and only from time to time he would dream of her with her touching smile as he dreamed of others. But more than a month went by, winter came into its own, and everything was still clear in his memory as though he had parted from Anna Sergeyevna only yesterday. And his memories glowed more and more vividly. When in the evening stillness the voices of his children preparing their lessons reached his study, or when he listened to a song or to an organ playing in a restaurant, or when the storm howled in the chimney, suddenly everything would rise up in his memory; what had happened on the pier and the early morning with the mist on the mountains, and the steamer coming from Feodosia, and the kisses. He would pace about his room a long time, remembering and smiling; then his memories passed into reveries, and in his imagination the past would mingle with what was to come. He did not dream of Anna Sergeyevna, but she followed him about everywhere and watched him. When he shut his eyes he saw her before him as though she were there in the flesh, and she seemed to him lovelier, younger, tenderer than she had been, and he imagined himself a finer man than he had been in Yalta. Of evenings she peered out at him from the bookcase, from the fireplace, from the corner—he heard her breathing, the caressing rustle of her clothes. In the street he followed the women with his eyes, looking for someone who resembled her.

Already he was tormented by a strong desire to share his memories with someone. But in his home it was impossible to talk of his love, and he had no one to talk to outside; certainly he could not confide in his tenants or in anyone at the bank. And what was there to talk about? He hadn't loved her then, had he? Had there been anything beautiful, poetical, edifying, or simply interesting in his relations with Anna Sergeyevna? And he was forced to talk vaguely of love, of women, and no one guessed what he meant; only his wife would twitch her black eyebrows and say, "The part of a philanderer does not suit you at all, Dimitry."

One evening, coming out of the physicians' club with an official with whom he had been playing cards, he could not resist saying:

"If you only knew what a fascinating woman I became acquainted with at Yalta!"

THE LADY WITH THE PET DOG

The official got into his sledge and was driving away, but turned suddenly and shouted:

"Dmitry Dmitrich!"

"What is it?"

"You were right this evening: the sturgeon was a bit high."

These words, so commonplace, for some reason moved Gurov to indignation, and struck him as degrading and unclean. What savage manners, what mugs! What stupid nights, what dull, humdrum days! Frenzied gambling, gluttony, drunkenness, continual talk always about the same thing! Futile pursuits and conversations always about the same topics take up the better part of one's time, the better part of one's strength, and in the end there is left a life clipped and wingless, an absurd mess, and there is no escaping or getting away from it—just as though one were in a madhouse or a prison.

Gurov, boiling with indignation, did not sleep all night. And he had a headache all the next day. And the following nights too he slept badly; he sat up in bed, thinking, or paced up and down his room. He was fed up with his children, fed up with the bank; he had no desire to go anywhere or to talk of anything.

In December during the holidays he prepared to take a trip and told his wife he was going to Petersburg to do what he could for a young friend—and he set off for S— What for? He did not know, himself. He wanted to see Anna Sergeyevna and talk with her, to arrange a rendezvous if possible.

He arrived at S— in the morning, and at the hotel took the best room, in which the floor was covered with gray army cloth, and on the table there was an inkstand,

ANTON CHEKHOV

gray with dust and topped by a figure on horseback, its hat in its raised hand and its head broken off. The porter gave him the necessary information: von Dideritz lived in a house of his own on Staro-Goncharnaya Street, not far from the hotel: he was rich and lived well and kept his own horses; everyone in the town knew him. The porter pronounced the name: "Dridiritz."

Without haste Gurov made his way to Staro-Goncharnaya Street and found the house. Directly opposite the house stretched a long gray fence studded with nails.

"A fence like that would make one run away," thought Gurov, looking now at the fence, now at the windows of the house.

He reflected: this was a holiday, and the husband was apt to be at home. And in any case, it would be tactless to go into the house and disturb her. If he were to send her a note, it might fall into her husband's hands, and that might spoil everything. The best thing was to rely on chance. And he kept walking up and down the street and along the fence, waiting for the chance. He saw a beggar go in at the gate and heard the dogs attack him; then an hour later he heard a piano, and the sound came to him faintly and indistinctly. Probably it was Anna Sergeyevna playing. The front door opened suddenly, and an old woman came out, followed by the familiar white Pomeranian. Gurov was on the point of calling to the dog, but his heart began beating violently, and in his excitement he could not remember the Pomeranian's name.

He kept walking up and down, and hated the gray fence more and more, and by now he thought irritably

THE LADY WITH THE PET DOG

that Anna Sergeyevna had forgotten him, and was perhaps already diverting herself with another man, and that that was very natural in a young woman who from morning till night had to look at that damn fence. He went back to his hotel room and sat on the couch for a long while, not knowing what to do, then he had dinner and a long nap.

"How stupid and annoying all this is!" he thought when he woke and looked at the dark windows: it was already evening. "Here I've had a good sleep for some reason. What am I going to do at night?"

He sat on the bed, which was covered with a cheap gray blanket of the kind seen in hospitals, and he twitted himself in his vexation:

"So there's your lady with the pet dog. There's your adventure. A nice place to cool your heels in."

That morning at the station a playbill in large letters had caught his eye. *The Geisha* was to be given for the first time. He thought of this and drove to the theater.

"It's quite possible that she goes to first nights," he thought.

The theater was full. As in all provincial theaters, there was a haze above the chandelier, the gallery was noisy and restless; in the front row, before the beginning of the performance the local dandies were standing with their hands clasped behind their backs; in the Governor's box the Governor's daughter, wearing a boa, occupied the front seat, while the Governor himself hid modestly behind the portiere and only his hands were visible; the curtain swayed; the orchestra was a long time tuning up. While the audience were coming in and taking their seats, Gurov scanned the faces eagerly.

Anna Sergeyevna, too, came in. She sat down in the third row, and when Gurov looked at her his heart contracted, and he understood clearly that in the whole world there was no human being so near, so precious, and so important to him; she, this little, undistinguished woman, lost in a provincial crowd, with a vulgar lorgnette in her hand, filled his whole life now, was his sorrow and his joy, the only happiness that he now desired for himself, and to the sounds of the bad orchestra, of the miserable local violins, he thought how lovely she was. He thought and dreamed.

A young man with small side-whiskers, very tall and stooped, came in with Anna Sergeyevna and sat down beside her; he nodded his head at every step and seemed to be bowing continually. Probably this was the husband whom at Yalta, in an access of bitter feeling, she had called a flunkey. And there really was in his lanky figure, his side-whiskers, his small bald patch, something of a flunkey's retiring manner; his smile was mawkish, and in his buttonhole there was an academic badge like a waiter's number.

During the first intermission the husband went out to have a smoke; she remained in her seat. Gurov, who was also sitting in the orchestra, went up to her and said in a shaky voice, with a forced smile:

"Good evening!"

She glanced at him and turned pale, then looked at him again in horror, unable to believe her eyes, and gripped the fan and the lorgnette tightly together in her hands, evidently trying to keep herself from faint-

THE LADY WITH THE PET DOG

ing. Both were silent. She was sitting, he was standing, frightened by her distress and not daring to take a seat beside her. The violins and the flute that were being tuned up sang out. He suddenly felt frightened: it seemed as if all the people in the boxes were looking at them. She got up and went hurriedly to the exit; he followed her, and both of them walked blindly along the corridors and up and down stairs, and figures in the uniforms prescribed for magistrates, teachers, and officials of the Department of Crown Lands, all wearing badges, flitted before their eyes, as did also ladies, and fur coats on hangers; they were conscious of drafts and the smell of stale tobacco. And Gurov, whose heart was beating violently, thought:

"Oh, Lord! Why are these people here and this orchestra!"

And at that instant he suddenly recalled how when he had seen Anna Sergeyevna off at the station he had said to himself that all was over between them and that they would never meet again. But how distant the end still was!

On the narrow, gloomy staircase over which it said "To the Amphitheatre," she stopped.

"How you frightened me!" she said, breathing hard, still pale and stunned. "Oh, how you frightened me! I am barely alive. Why did you come? Why?"

"But do understand, Anna, do understand——" he said hurriedly, under his breath. "I implore you, do understand——"

She looked at him with fear, with entreaty, with love; she looked at him intently, to keep his features more distinctly in her memory.

ANTON CHEKHOV

"I suffer so," she went on, not listening to him. "All this time I have been thinking of nothing but you; I live only by the thought of you. And I wanted to forget, to forget; but why, oh, why have you come?"

On the landing above them two high school boys were looking down and smoking, but it was all the same to Gurov; he drew Anna Sergeyevna to him and began kissing her face and her hands.

"What are you doing, what are you doing!" she was saying in horror, pushing him away. "We have lost our senses. Go away today; go away at once— I conjure you by all that is sacred, I implore you— People are coming this way!"

Someone was walking up the stairs.

"You must leave," Anna Sergeyevna went on in a whisper. "Do you hear, Dmitry Dmitrich? I will come and see you in Moscow. I have never been happy; I am unhappy now, and I never, never shall be happy, never! So don't make me suffer still more! I swear I'll come to Moscow. But now let us part. My dear, good, precious one, let us part!"

She pressed his hand and walked rapidly downstairs, turning to look round at him, and from her eyes he could see that she really was unhappy. Gurov stood for a while, listening, then when all grew quiet, he found his coat and left the theater.

IV

And Anna Sergeyevna began coming to see him in Moscow. Once every two or three months she left

THE LADY WITH THE PET DOG

S— telling her husband that she was going to consult a doctor about a woman's ailment from which she was suffering—and her husband did and did not believe her. When she arrived in Moscow she would stop at the Slavyansky Bazar Hotel, and at once send a man in a red cap to Gurov. Gurov came to see her, and no one in Moscow knew of it.

Once he was going to see her in this way on a winter morning (the messenger had come the evening before and not found him in). With him walked his daughter, whom he wanted to take to school; it was on the way. Snow was coming down in big wet flakes.

"It's three degrees above zero, and yet it's snowing." Gurov was saying to his daughter. "But this temperature prevails only on the surface of the earth; in the upper layers of the atmosphere there is quite a different temperature."

"And why doesn't it thunder in winter, papa?"

He explained that, too. He talked, thinking all the while that he was on his way to a rendezvous, and no living soul knew of it, and probably no one would ever know. He had two lives, an open one, seen and known by all who needed to know it, full of conventional truth and conventional falsehood, exactly like the lives of his friends and acquaintances; and another life that went on in secret. And through some strange, perhaps accidental, combination of circumstances, everything that was of interest and importance to him, everything that was essential to him, everything about which he felt sincerely and did not deceive himself, everything that constituted the core of his life, was going on concealed from others; while all that was false, the shell in which

ANTON CHEKHOV

he hid to cover the truth—his work at the bank, for instance, his discussions at the club, his references to the "inferior race," his appearances at anniversary celebrations with his wife—all that went on in the open. Judging others by himself, he did not believe what he saw, and always fancied that every man led his real, most interesting life under cover of secrecy as under cover of night. The personal life of every individual is based on secrecy, and perhaps it is partly for that reason that civilized man is so nervously anxious that personal privacy should be respected.

Having taken his daughter to school, Gurov went on to the Slavyansky Bazar Hotel. He took off his fur coat in the lobby, went upstairs, and knocked gently at the door. Anna Sergeyevna, wearing his favorite gray dress, exhausted by the journey and by waiting, had been expecting him since the previous evening. She was pale, and looked at him without a smile, and he had hardly entered when she flung herself on his breast. That kiss was a long, lingering one, as though they had not seen one another for two years.

"Well, darling, how are you getting on there?" he asked. "What news?"

"Wait; I'll tell you in a moment— I can't speak."

She could not speak; she was crying. She turned away from him, and pressed her handkerchief to her eyes.

"Let her have her cry; meanwhile I'll sit down," he thought, and he seated himself in an armchair.

Then he rang and ordered tea, and while he was having his tea she remained standing at the window with her back to him. She was crying out of sheer agita-

THE LADY WITH THE PET DOG

tion, in the sorrowful consciousness that their life was so sad; that they could only see each other in secret and had to hide from people like thieves! Was it not a broken life?

"Come, stop now, dear!" he said.

It was plain to him that this love of theirs would not be over soon, that the end of it was not in sight. Anna Sergeyevna was growing more and more attached to him. She adored him, and it was unthinkable to tell her that their love was bound to come to an end some day; besides, she would not have believed it!

He went up to her and took her by the shoulders, to fondle her and say something diverting, and at that moment he caught sight of himself in the mirror.

His hair was already beginning to turn gray. And it seemed odd to him that he had grown so much older in the last few years, and lost his looks. The shoulders on which his hands rested were warm and heaving. He felt compassion for this life, still so warm and lovely, but probably already about to begin to fade and wither like his own. Why did she love him so much? He always seemed to women different from what he was, and they loved in him not himself, but the man whom their imagination created and whom they had been eagerly seeking all their lives; and afterwards, when they saw their mistake, they loved him nevertheless. And not one of them had been happy with him. In the past he had met women, come together with them, parted from them, but he had never once loved; it was anything you please, but not love. And only now when his head was gray he had fallen in love, really, truly— for the first time in his life.

ANTON CHEKHOV

Anna Sergeyevna and he loved each other as people do who are very close and intimate, like man and wife, like tender friends; it seemed to them that Fate itself had meant them for one another, and they could not understand why he had a wife and she a husband; and it was as though they were a pair of migratory birds, male and female, caught and forced to live in different cages. They forgave each other what they were ashamed of in their past, they forgave everything in the present, and felt that this love of theirs had altered them both.

Formerly in moments of sadness he had soothed himself with whatever logical arguments came into his head, but now he no longer cared for logic; he felt profound compassion, he wanted to be sincere and tender.

"Give it up now, my darling," he said. "You've had your cry; that's enough. Let us have a talk now, we'll think up something."

Then they spent a long time taking counsel together, they talked of how to avoid the necessity for secrecy, for deception, for living in different cities, and not seeing one another for long stretches of time. How could they free themselves from these intolerable fetters?

"How? How?" he asked, clutching his head. "How?"

And it seemed as though in a little while the solution would be found, and then a new and glorious life would begin; and it was clear to both of them that the end was still far off, and that what was to be most complicated and difficult for them was only just beginning.

In the Zoo

First person narration. The narrator is not a principal actor in the episode that forms the main body of the story, but is an involved witness to it. As the story broadens and the *pattern* of the corruption of the dog is repeated in the lives of the sisters, we see that it is really their story after all.

Narration in the first person permits considerable fluidity in the handling of time. The *scene* that opens the story is continued after a very long *flashback,* thus forming a kind of *envelope* around the material from a past time.

The basic realism of the story is heightened and modulated by a rhetorical style. The mixture of gaiety and despair that seems almost to be the quality of the narrator's *voice* contributes much to the special *tone.*

Note the smooth shifting of the *focus of interest* from animals to humans, to animals, to humans. The animals are *symbols,* but only in a limited, well-controlled fashion. That is, they represent something to the characters but have no other particular burden of meaning.

117

In the Zoo

by

JEAN STAFFORD

Keening harshly in his senility, the blind polar bear slowly and ceaselessly shakes his head in the stark heat of the July and mountain noon. His open eyes are blue. No one stops to look at him; an old farmer, in passing, sums up the old bear's situation by observing, with a ruthless chuckle, that he is a "back number." Patient and despairing, he sits on his yellowed haunches on the central rock of his pool, his huge toy paws wearing short boots of mud.

The grizzlies to the right of him, a conventional family of father and mother and two spring cubs, alternately play the clown and sleep. There is a blustery, scoundrelly, half-likable bravado in the manner of the black bear on the polar's left; his name, according to the legend on his cage, is Clancy, and he is a rough-and-tumble, brawling blowhard, thundering continually as he paces back and forth, or pauses to face his audience of children and mothers and release from his great, gray-tongued mouth a perfectly Vesuvian roar. If he were to be

JEAN STAFFORD

reincarnated in human form, he would be a man of action, possibly a football coach, probably a politician. One expects to see his black hat hanging from a branch of one of his trees; at any moment he will light a cigar.

The polar bear's next-door neighbors are not the only ones who offer so sharp and sad a contrast to him. Across a reach of scrappy grass and litter is the convocation of conceited monkeys, burrowing into each other's necks and chests for fleas, picking their noses with their long, black, finicky fingers, swinging by their gifted tails on the flying trapeze, screaming bloody murder. Even when they mourn—one would think the male orangutan was on the very brink of suicide— they are comedians; they only fake depression, for they are firmly secure in their rambunctious tribalism and in their appalling insight and contempt. Their flibbertigibbet gambolling is a sham, and, stealthily and shiftily, they are really watching the pitiful polar bear ("Back number," they quote the farmer. "That's *his* number all right," they snigger), and the windy black bear ("Life of the party. Gasbag. Low I.Q.," they note scornfully on his dossier), and the stupid, bourgeois grizzlies ("It's feed the face and hit the sack for them," the monkeys say). And they are watching my sister and me, two middle-aged women, as we sit on a bench between the exhibits, eating popcorn, growing thirsty. We are thoughtful.

A chance remark of Daisy's a few minutes before has turned us to memory and meditation. "I don't know why," she said, "but that poor blind bear reminds me of Mr. Murphy." The name "Mr. Murphy" at once returned us both to childhood, which has little

IN THE ZOO

to do with hunger; it is not so much food as a sacrament, and in tribute to our sisterliness and our friendliness I break the silence to say that this is the best popcorn I have ever eaten in my life. The extravagance of my statement instantly makes me feel self-indulgent, and for some time I uneasily avoid looking at the blind bear. My sister does not agree or disagree; she simply says that popcorn is the only food she has ever really liked. For a long time, then, we eat without a word, but I know, because I know her well and know her similarity to me, that Daisy is thinking what I am thinking; both of us are mournfully remembering Mr. Murphy, who, at one time in our lives, was our only friend.

This zoo is in Denver, a city that means nothing to my sister and me except as a place to take or meet trains. Daisy lives two hundred miles farther west, and it is her custom when my every-other-year visit with her is over, to come across the mountains to see me off on my eastbound train. We know almost no one here, and because our stays are short, we have never bothered to learn the town in more than the most desultory way. We know the Burlington uptown office and the respectable hotels, a restaurant or two, the Union Station, and, beginning today, the zoo in the city park.

But since the moment that Daisy named Mr. Murphy by name our situation in Denver has been only corporeal; our minds and our hearts are in Adams, fifty miles north, and we are seeing, under the white sun at its pitiless meridian, the streets of that ugly town, its parks and trees and bridges, the bandstand in its dreary park, the roads that lead away from it, west to the mountains and east to the plains, its mongrel

JEAN STAFFORD

and multitudinous churches, its high school shaped like
a loaf of bread, the campus of its college, an oasis of
which we had no experience except to walk through it
now and then, eying the woodbine on the impressive
buildings. These things are engraved forever on our
minds with a legibility so insistent that you have only
to say the name of the town aloud to us to rip the rinds
from our nerves and leave us exposed in terror and
humiliation.

We have supposed in later years that Adams was not
so bad as all that, and we know that we magnified its
ugliness because we looked upon it as the extension of
the possessive, unloving, scornful, complacent foster
mother, Mrs. Placer, to whom, at the death of our
parents within a month of each other, we were sent like
Dickensian grotesqueries—cowardly, weak-stomached,
given to tears, backward in school. Daisy was ten and
I was eight when, unaccompanied, we made the long
trip from Marblehead to our benefactress, whom we
had never seen and, indeed, never heard of until the
pastor of our church came to tell us of the arrangement our father had made on his deathbed, seconded by
our mother on hers. This man, whose name and face I
have forgotten and whose parting speeches to us I
have not forgiven, tried to dry our tears with talk of
Indians and of buffaloes; he spoke, however, at much
greater length, and in preaching cadences, of the
Christian goodness of Mrs. Placer. She was, he said,
childless and fond of children, and for many years
she had been a widow, after the lingering demise of
her tubercular husband, for whose sake she had moved
to the Rocky Mountains. For his support and costly

121

IN THE ZOO

medical care, she had run a boarding house, and after his death, since he had left her nothing, she was obliged to continue running it. She had been a girlhood friend of our paternal grandmother, and our father, in the absence of responsible relatives, had made her the beneficiary of his life insurance on the condition that she lodge and rear us. The pastor, with a frankness remarkable considering that he was talking to children, explained to us that our father had left little more than a drop in the bucket for our care, and he enjoined us to give Mrs. Placer, in return for her hospitality and sacrifice, courteous help and eternal thanks. "Sacrifice" was a word we were never allowed to forget.

And thus it was, in grief for our parents, that we came cringing to the dry Western town and to the house where Mrs. Placer lived, a house in which the square, uncushioned furniture was cruel and the pictures on the walls were either dour or dire and the lodgers, who lived in the upper floors among shadowy wardrobes and chiffoniers, had come through the years to resemble their landlady in appearance as well as in deportment.

After their ugly-colored evening meal, Gran—as she bade us call her—and her paying guests would sit, rangy and aquiline, rocking on the front porch on spring and summer and autumn nights, tasting their delicious grievances; those slights delivered by ungrateful sons and daughters, those impudences committed by trolley-car conductors and uppity salesgirls in the ready-to-wear, all those slurs and calculated elbow-jostlings that were their daily crucifixion and their staff of life. We little girls, washing the dishes in the

JEAN STAFFORD

cavernous kitchen, listened to their even, martyred voices, fixed like leeches to their solitary subject and their solitary creed—that life was essentially a matter of being done in, let down, and swindled.

At regular intervals, Mrs. Placer, chairwoman of the victims, would say, "Of course, I don't care; I just have to laugh," and then would tell a shocking tale of an intricate piece of skulduggery perpetrated against her by someone she did not even know. Sometimes, with her avid, partial jury sitting there on the porch behind the bitter hopvines in the heady mountain air, the cases she tried involved Daisy and me, and, listening, we travailed, hugging each other, whispering, "I wish she wouldn't! Oh, how did she find out?" How *did* she? Certainly we never told her when we were snubbed or chosen last on teams, never admitted to a teacher's scolding or to the hoots of laughter that greeted us when we bit on silly, unfair jokes. But she knew. She knew about the slumber parties we were not invited to, the beefsteak fries from which we were pointedly left out; she knew that the singing teacher had said in so many words that I could not carry a tune in a basket and that the sewing superintendent had said that Daisy's fingers were all thumbs. With our teeth chattering in the cold of our isolation, we would hear her protestant, litigious voice defending our right to be orphans, paupers, wholly dependent on her—except for the really ridiculous pittance from our father's life insurance—when it was all she could do to make ends meet. She did not care, but she had to laugh that people in general were so small-minded that they looked down on fatherless, motherless waifs like us and, by association, looked down on her.

IN THE ZOO

It seemed funny to her that people gave her no credit for taking on these sickly youngsters who were not even kin but only the grandchildren of a friend.

If a child with braces on her teeth came to play with us, she was, according to Gran, slyly lording it over us because our teeth were crooked, but there was no money to have them straightened. And what could be the meaning of our being asked to come for supper at the doctor's house? Were the doctor and his la-di-da New York wife and those pert girls with their solid-gold barrettes and their Shetland pony going to shame her poor darlings? Or shame their poor Gran by making them sorry to come home to the plain but honest life that was all she could provide for them?

There was no stratum of society not reeking with the effluvium of fraud and pettifoggery. And the school system was almost the worst of all: if we could not understand fractions, was that not our teacher's fault? And therefore what right had she to give us F? It was as plain as a pikestaff to Gran that the teacher was only covering up her own inability to teach. It was unlikely, too—highly unlikely—that it was by accident that time and time again the free medical clinic was closed for the day just as our names were about to be called out, so that nothing was done about our bad tonsils, which meant that we were repeatedly sick in the winter, with Gran fetching and carrying for us, climbing those stairs a jillion times a day with her game leg and her heart that was none too strong.

Steeped in these mists of accusation and hidden plots and double meanings, Daisy and I grew up like worms. I think no one could have withstood the atmosphere in that house where everyone trod on eggs that a little bird had told them were bad. They spied on one another, whispered behind doors, conjectured, drew parallels beginning "With all due respect . . ." or "It is a matter of indifference to *me* but . . ." The vigilantes patrolled our town by day, and by night returned to lay their goodies at their priestess's feet and wait for her oracular interpretation of the innards of the butcher, the baker, the candlestick maker, the soda jerk's girl, and the barber's unnatural deaf white cat.

Consequently, Daisy and I also became suspicious. But it was suspicion of ourselves that made us mope and weep and grimace with self-judgment. Why were we not happy when Gran had sacrificed herself to the bone for us? Why did we not cut dead the paper boy who had called her a filthy name? Why did we persist in our willful friendliness with the grocer who had tried, unsuccessfully, to overcharge her on a case of pork and beans?

Our friendships were nervous and surreptitious; we sneaked and lied, and as our hungers sharpened, our debasement deepened; we were pitied; we were shifty-eyed, always on the lookout for Mrs. Placer or one of her tattletale lodgers; we were hypocrites.

Nevertheless, one thin filament of instinct survived, and Daisy and I in time found asylum in a small menagerie down by the railroad tracks. It belonged to a gentle alcoholic ne'er-do-well, who did nothing all day long but drink bathtub gin in rickeys and play solitaire and smile to himself and talk to his animals. He had a little, stunted red vixen and a deodorized skunk, a parrot from Tahiti that spoke Parisian French,

125

IN THE ZOO

a woebegone coyote, and two capuchin monkeys, so serious and humanized, so small and sad and sweet, and so religious-looking with their tonsured heads that it was impossible not to think their gibberish was really an ordered language with a grammar that someday some philologist would understand.

Gran knew about our visits to Mr. Murphy and she did not object, for it gave her keen pleasure to excoriate him when we came home. His vice was not a matter of guesswork; it was an established fact that he was half-seas over from dawn till midnight. "With the black Irish," said Gran, "the taste for drink is taken in with the mother's milk and is never mastered. Oh, I know all about those promises to join the temperance movement and not to touch another drop. The way to Hell is paved with good intentions."

We were still little girls when we discovered Mr. Murphy, before the shattering disease of adolescence was to make our bones and brains ache even more painfully than before, and we loved him and we hoped to marry him when we grew up. We loved him, and loved his monkeys to exactly the same degree and in exactly the same way; they were husbands and fathers and brothers, these three little, ugly, dark, secret men who minded their own business and let us mind ours. If we stuck our fingers through the bars of the cage, the monkeys would sometimes take them in their tight, tiny hands and look into our faces with a tentative, somehow absent-minded sorrow, as if they terribly regretted that they could not place us but were glad to see us all the same. Mr. Murphy, playing a solitaire game of cards called "once in a blue moon" on a kitchen

JEAN STAFFORD

table in his back yard beside the pens, would occasionally look up and blink his beautiful blue eyes and say, "You're peaches to make over my wee friends. I love you for it." There was nothing demanding in his voice, and nothing sticky; on his lips the word "love" was jocose and forthright, it had no strings attached. We would sit on either side of him and watch him regiment his ranks of cards and stop to drink as deeply as if he were dying of thirst and wave to his animals and say to them, "Yes, lads, you're dandies."

Because Mr. Murphy was as reserved with us as the capuchins were, as courteously noncommittal, we were surprised one spring day when he told us that he had a present for us, which he hoped Mrs. Placer would let us keep; it was a puppy, for whom the owner had asked him to find a home—half collie and half Labrador retriever, blue-blooded on both sides.

"You might tell Mrs. Placer"—he said, smiling at the name, for Gran was famous in the town—"you might tell Mrs. Placer," said Mr. Murphy, "that this lad will make a fine watchdog. She'll never have to fear for her spoons again. Or her honor." The last he said to himself, not laughing but tucking his chin into his collar; lines sprang to the corners of his eyes. He would not let us see the dog, whom we could hear yipping and squealing inside his shanty, for he said that our disappointment would weigh on his conscience if we lost our hearts to the fellow and then could not have him for our own.

That evening at supper, we told Gran about Mr. Murphy's present. A dog? In the first place, why a dog? Was it possible that the news had reached Mr. Murphy's

IN THE ZOO

ears that Gran had just this very day finished planting her spring garden, the very thing that a rampageous dog would have in his mind to destroy? What sex was it? A male! Females, she had heard, were more trustworthy; males roved and came home smelling of skunk; such a consideration as this, of course, would not have crossed Mr. Murphy's fuddled mind. Was this young male dog housebroken? We had not asked? That was the limit!

Gran appealed to her followers, too raptly fascinated by Mr. Murphy's machinations to eat their Harvard beets. "Am I being farfetched or does it strike you as decidedly queer that Mr. Murphy is trying to fob off on my little girls a young cur that has not been trained?" she asked them. "If it were housebroken, he would have said so, so I feel it is safe to assume that it is not. Perhaps cannot *be* housebroken. I've heard of such cases."

The fantasy spun on, richly and rapidly, with all the skilled helping hands at work at once. The dog was tangibly in the room with us, shedding his hair, biting his fleas, shaking rain off himself to splatter the walls, dragging some dreadful carcass across the floor, chewing up slippers, knocking over chairs with his tail, gobbling the chops from the platter, barking, biting, fathering, fighting, smelling to high heaven of carrion, staining the rug with his muddy feet, scratching the floor with his claws. He developed rabies; he bit a child, two children! Three! Everyone in town! And Gran and her poor darlings went to jail for harboring this murderous, odoriferous, drunk, Roman Catholic dog.

And yet, astoundingly enough, she came around to

agreeing to let us have the dog. It was, as Mr. Murphy had predicted, the word "watchdog" that deflected the course of the trial. The moment Daisy uttered it, Gran halted, marshalling her reverse march; while she rallied and tacked and reconnoitred, she sent us to the kitchen for the dessert. And by the time this course was under way, the uses of a dog, the enormous potentialities for investigation and law enforcement in a dog trained by Mrs. Placer, were being minutely and passionately scrutinized by the eight upright bloodhounds sitting at the table wolfing their brown Betty as if it were fresh-killed rabbit. The dog now sat at attention beside his mistress, fiercely alert, ears cocked, nose aquiver, the protector of widows, of orphans, of lonely people who had no homes. He made short shrift of burglars, homicidal maniacs, Peeping Toms, gypsies, bogus missionaries, Fuller Brush men with a risqué spiel. He went to the store and brought back groceries, retrieved the evening paper from the awkward place the boy had meanly thrown it, rescued cripples from burning houses, saved children from drowning, heeled at command, begged, lay down, stood up, sat, jumped through a hoop, ratted.

Both times—when he was a ruffian of the blackest delinquency and then a pillar of society—he was full-grown in his prefiguration, and when Laddy appeared on the following day, small, unsteady, and whimpering lonesomely, Gran and her lodgers were taken aback; his infant, clumsy paws embarrassed them, his melting eyes were unapropos. But it could never be said of Mrs. Placer, as Mrs. Placer her own self said, that she was a woman who went back on her word, and her darlings were going to have their dog, soft-headed and feckless as he might be. All the first night, in his carton in the kitchen, he wailed for his mother, and in the morning, it was true, he had made a shambles of the room— fouled the floor, and pulled off the tablecloth together with a ketchup bottle, so that thick gore lay everywhere. At breakfast, the lodgers confessed they had had a most amusing night, for it had actually been funny the way the dog had been determined not to let anyone get a wink of sleep. After that first night, Laddy slept in our room, receiving from us, all through our delighted, sleepless nights, pats and embraces and kisses and whispers. He was our baby, our best friend, the smartest, prettiest, nicest dog in the entire wide world. Our soft and rapid blandishments excited him to yelp at us in pleased bewilderment, and then we would playfully grasp his muzzle, so that he would snarl, deep in his throat like an adult dog, and shake his head violently, and, when we freed him, nip us smartly with great good will.

He was an intelligent and genial dog and we trained him quickly. He steered clear of Gran's radishes and lettuce after she had several times given him a brisk comeuppance with a strap across the rump, and he soon left off chewing shoes and the laundry on the line, and he outgrew his babyish whining. He grew like a weed; he lost his spherical softness, and his coat, which had been sooty fluff, came in stiff and rusty black; his nose grew aristocratically long, and his clever, pointed ears stood at attention. He was all bronzy, lustrous black except for an Elizabethan ruff of white and a tip of white at the end of his perky tail. No one could deny

JEAN STAFFORD

that he was exceptionally handsome and that he had, as well, great personal charm and style. He escorted Daisy and me to school in the morning, laughing interiorly out of the enormous pleasure of his life as he gracefully cantered ahead of us, distracted occasionally by his private interest in smells or unfamiliar beings in the grass but, on the whole, engrossed in his role of chaperon. He made friends easily with other dogs, and sometimes he went for a long hunting weekend into the mountains with a huge and bossy old red hound named Mess, who had been on the county most of his life and had made a good thing of it, particularly at the fire station.

It was after one of these three-day excursions into the high country that Gran took Laddy in hand. He had come back spent and filthy, his coat a mass of cockleburs and ticks, his eyes bloodshot, loud *râles* in his chest; for half a day he lay motionless before the front door like someone in a hangover, his groaning eyes explicitly saying "Oh, for God's sake, leave me be" when we offered him food or bowls of water. Gran was disapproving, then affronted, and finally furious. Not, of course, with Laddy, since all inmates of her house enjoyed immunity, but with Mess, whose caddish character, together with that of his nominal masters, the firemen, she examined closely under a strong light, with an air of detachment, with her not caring but her having, all the same, to laugh. A lodger who occupied the back west room had something to say about the fire chief and his nocturnal visits to a certain house occupied by a certain group of young women, too near the same age to be sisters and too old to be the daughters of

IN THE ZOO

the woman who claimed to be their mother. What a story! The exophthalmic librarian—she lived in one of the front rooms—had some interesting insinuations to make about the deputy marshal, who had borrowed, significantly, she thought, a book on hypnotism. She also knew—she was, of course, in a most useful position in the town, and from her authoritative pen in the middle of the library her mammiform and azure eyes and her eager ears missed nothing—that the fire chief's wife was not as scrupulous as she might be when she was keeping score on bridge night at the Sorosis.

There was little at the moment that Mrs. Placer and her disciples could do to save the souls of the Fire Department and their families, and therefore save the town from holocaust (a very timid boarder—a Mr. Beaver, a newcomer who was not to linger long—had sniffed throughout this recitative as if he were smelling burning flesh), but at least the unwholesome bond between Mess and Laddy could and would be severed once and for all. Gran looked across the porch at Laddy, who lay stretched at full length in the darkest corner, shuddering and baying abortively in his throat as he chased jack rabbits in his dreams, and she said, "A dog can have morals like a human." With this declaration Laddy's randy, manly holidays were finished. It may have been telepathy that woke him; he lifted his heavy head from his paws, laboriously got up, hesitated for a moment, and then padded languidly across the porch to Gran. He stood docilely beside her chair, head down, tail drooping as if to say, "O.K. Mrs. Placer, show me how and I'll walk the straight and narrow."

The very next day, Gran changed Laddy's name to

JEAN STAFFORD

Caesar, as being more dignified, and a joke was made at the supper table that he had come, seen, and conquered Mrs. Placer's heart—for within her circle, where the magnanimity she lavished upon her orphans was daily demonstrated, Mrs. Placer's heart was highly thought of. On that day also, although we did not know it yet, Laddy ceased to be our dog. Before many weeks passed, indeed, he ceased to be anyone we had ever known. A week or so after he became Caesar, he took up residence in her room, sleeping alongside her bed. She broke him of the habit of taking us to school (temptation to low living was rife along those streets; there was a chow—well, never mind) by the simple expedient of chaining him to a tree as soon as she got up in the morning. This discipline, together with the stamina-building cuffs she gave his sensitive ears from time to time, gradually but certainly remade his character. From a sanguine, affectionate, easygoing Gael (with the fits of melancholy that alternated with the larkiness), he turned into an overbearing, military, efficient, loud-voiced Teuton. His bark, once wide of range, narrowed to one dark, glottal tone.

Soon the paper boy flatly refused to serve our house after Caesar efficiently removed the bicycle clip from his pants leg; the skin was not broken, or even bruised, but it was a matter of principle with the boy. The milkman approached the back door in a seizure of shakes like St. Vitus's dance. The meter-men, the coal men, and the garbage collector crossed themselves if they were Catholics and, if they were not, tried whistling in the dark. "Good boy, good Caesar," they carolled, and, unctuously lying, they said they knew his bark was

IN THE ZOO

worse than his bite, knowing full well that it was not, considering the very nasty nip, requiring stiches, he had given a representative of the Olson Rug Company, who had had the folly to pat him on the head. Caesar did not molest the lodgers, but he disdained them and he did not brook being personally addressed by anyone except Gran. One night, he wandered into the dining room, appearing to be in search of something he had mislaid, and, for some reason that no one was ever able to divine, suddenly stook stock-still and gave the easily upset Mr. Beaver a long and penetrating look. Mr. Beaver, trembling from head to toe, stammered, "Why—er, hello there, Caesar, old boy, old boy," and Caesar charged. For a moment, it was touch and go, but Gran saved Mr. Beaver, only to lose him an hour later when he departed, bag and baggage, for the Y.M.C.A. This rout and the consequent loss of revenue would more than likely have meant Caesar's downfall and his deportation to the pound if it had not been that a newly widowed druggist, very irascible and very much Gran's style, had applied for a room in her house a week or so before, and now he moved in delightedly, as if he were coming home.

Finally, the police demanded that Caesar be muzzled and they warned that if he committed any major crime again—they cited the case of the Olson man—he would be shot on sight. Mrs. Placer, although she had no respect for the law, knowing as much as she did about its agents, obeyed. She obeyed, that is, in part; she put the muzzle on Caesar for a few hours a day, usually early in the morning when the traffic was light and before the deliveries had started, but the rest of the time his powerful jaws and dazzling white sabre teeth were free and snapping. There was between these two such preternatural rapport, such an impressive conjugation of suspicion, that he, sensing the approach of a policeman, could convey instantly to her the immediate necessity of clapping his nose cage on. And the policeman, sent out on the complaint of a terrorized neighbor, would be greeted by this law-abiding pair at the door.

Daisy and I wished we were dead. We were divided between hating Caesar and loving Laddy, and we could not give up the hope that something, someday, would change him back into the loving animal he had been before he was appointed vice-president of the Placerites. Now at the meetings after supper on the porch he took an active part, standing rigidly at Gran's side except when she sent him on an errand. He carried out these assignments not with the air of a servant but with that of an accomplice. "Get me the paper, Caesar," she would say to him, and he, dismayingly intelligent and a shade smart-alecky, would open the screen door by himself and in a minute come back with the *Bulletin*, from which Mrs. Placer would then read an item, like the Gospel of the day, and then read between the lines of it, scandalized.

In the deepening of our woe and our bereavement and humiliation, we mutely appealed to Mr. Murphy. We did not speak outright to him, for Mr. Murphy lived in a state of indirection, and often when he used the pronoun "I," he seemed to be speaking of someone standing a little to the left of him, but we went to see him and his animals each day during the sad summer, taking what comfort we could from the cozy, quiet

IN THE ZOO

indolence of his back yard, where small black eyes encountered ours politely and everyone was half asleep. When Mr. Murphy inquired about Laddy in his bland, inattentive way, looking for a stratagem whereby to shift the queen of hearts into position by the king, we would say, "Oh, he's fine," or "Laddy is a nifty dog." And Mr. Murphy, reverently slaking the thirst that was his talent and his concubine, would murmur, "I'm glad."

We wanted to tell him, we wanted his help, or at least his sympathy, but how could we cloud his sunny world? It was awful to see Mr. Murphy ruffled. Up in the calm clouds as he generally was, he could occasionally be brought to earth with a thud, as we had seen and heard one day. Not far from his house, there lived a bad, troublemaking boy of twelve, who was forever hanging over the fence trying to teach the parrot obscene words. He got nowhere, for she spoke no English and she would flabbergast him with her cold eye and sneer, *"Tant pis."* One day, this boorish fellow went too far; he suddenly shot his head over the fence like a jack-in-the-box and aimed a water pistol at the skunk's face. Mr. Murphy leaped to his feet in a scarlet rage; he picked up a stone and threw it accurately, hitting the boy square in the back, so hard that he fell right down in a mud puddle and lay there kicking and squalling and, as it turned out, quite badly hurt. "If you ever come back here again, I'll kill you!" roared Mr. Murphy. I think he meant it, for I have seldom seen an anger so resolute, so brilliant, and so voluble. "How dared he!" he cried, scrambling into Mallow's cage to hug and pet and soothe her. "He must

JEAN STAFFORD

be absolutely mad! He must be the Devil!" He did not go back to his game after that but paced the yard, swearing a blue streak and only pausing to croon to his animals, now as frightened by him as they had been by the intruder, and to drink straight from the bottle, not bothering with fixings. We were fascinated by this unfamiliar side of Mr. Murphy, but we did not want to see it ever again, for his face had grown so dangerously purple and the veins of his forehead seemed ready to burst and his eyes looked scorched. He was the closest thing to a maniac we had ever seen. So we did not tell him about Laddy; what he did not know would not hurt him, although it was hurting us, throbbing in us like a great, bleating wound.

But eventually Mr. Murphy heard about our dog's conversion, one night at the pool hall, which he visited from time to time when he was seized with a rare but compelling garrulity, and the next afternoon when he asked us how Laddy was and we replied that he was fine, he tranquilly told us, as he deliberated whether to move the jack of clubs now or to bide his time, that we were sweet girls but we were lying in our teeth. He did not seem at all angry but only interested, and all the while he questioned us, he went on about his business with the gin and the hearts and spades and diamonds and clubs. It rarely happened that he won the particular game he was playing, but that day he did, and when he saw all the cards laid out in their ideal pattern, he leaned back, looking disappointed, and he said, "I'm damned." He then scooped up the cards, in a gesture unusually quick and tidy for him, stacked them together, and bound them with a rubber band.

IN THE ZOO

Then he began to tell us what he thought of Gran. He grew as loud and apoplectic as he had been that other time, and though he kept repeating that he knew *we* were innocent and he put not a shred of the blame on us, we were afraid he might suddenly change his mind, and, and, speechless, we cowered against the monkeys' cage. In dread, the monkeys clutched the fingers we offered to them and made soft, protesting noises, as if to say, "Oh, stop it, Murphy! Our nerves!"

As quickly as it had started, the tantrum ended. Mr. Murphy paled to his normal complexion and said calmly that the only practical thing was to go and have it out with Mrs. Placer. "At once," he added, although he said he bitterly feared that it was too late and there would be no exorcising the fiend from Laddy's misused spirit. And because he had given the dog to us and not to her, he required that we go along with him, stick up for our rights, stand on our mettle, get up our Irish, and give the old bitch something to put in her pipe and smoke.

Oh, it was hot that day! We walked in a kind of delirium through the simmer, where only the grasshoppers had the energy to move, and I remember wondering if ether smelled like the gin on Mr. Murphy's breath. Daisy and I, in one way or another, were going to have our gizzards cut out along with our hearts and our souls and our pride, and I wished I were as drunk as Mr. Murphy, who swam effortlessly through the heat, his lips parted comfortably, his eyes half closed. When we turned in to the path at Gran's house, my blood began to scald my veins. It was so futile and so dangerous and so absurd. Here we were on a high moral mission, two draggletailed, gumptionless little girls and

a toper whom no one could take seriously, partly because he was little more than a gurgling bottle of booze
and partly because of the clothes he wore. He was a
sight, as he always was when he was out of his own
yard. There, somehow, in the carefree disorder, his
clothes did not look especially strange, but on the
streets of the town, in the barbershop or the post office
or on Gran's path, they were fantastic. He wore a pair
of hound's-tooth pants, old but maintaining a vehe-
ment pattern, and with them he wore a collarless blue
flannelette shirt. His hat was the silliest of all, because
it was a derby three sizes too big. And as if Shannon,
too, was a part of his funny-paper costume, the elder
capuchin rode on his shoulder, tightly embracing his
thin red neck.

Gran and Caesar were standing side by side behind
the screen door, looking as if they had been expecting
us all along. For a moment, Gran and Mr. Murphy
faced each other across the length of weedy brick between the gate and the front porch, and no one spoke.
Gran took no notice at all of Daisy and me. She adjusted her eyeglasses, using both hands, and then looked
down at Caesar and matter-of-factly asked, "Do you
want out?"

Caesar flung himself full-length upon the screen and
it sprang open like a jaw. I ran to meet and head him
off, and Daisy threw a library book at his head, but he
was on Mr. Murphy in one split second and had his
monkey off his shoulder and had broken Shannon's
neck in two shakes. He would have gone on nuzzling
and mauling and growling over the corpse for hours if
Gran had not marched out of the house and down the

path and slapped him lightly on the flank and said, in a voice that could not have deceived an idiot, "Why, Caesar, you scamp! You've hurt Mr. Murphy's monkey! Aren't you ashamed!"

Hurt the monkey! In one final, apologetic shudder, the life was extinguished from the little fellow. Bloody and covered with slather, Shannon lay with his arms suppliantly stretched over his head, his leather fingers curled into loose, helpless fists. His hind legs and his tail lay limp and helter-skelter on the path. And Mr. Murphy, all of a sudden reeling drunk, burst into the kind of tears that Daisy and I knew well—the kind that time alone could stop. We stood aghast in the dark-red sunset, killed by our horror and our grief for Shannon and our unforgivable disgrace. We stood upright in a dead faint, and an eon passed before Mr. Murphy picked up Shannon's body and wove away, sobbing, "I don't believe it! I don't *believe* it!"

The very next day, again at morbid, heavy sunset, Caesar died in violent convulsions, knocking down two tall hollyhocks in his throes. Long after his heart had stopped, his right hind leg continued to jerk in aimless reflex. Madly methodical, Mr. Murphy had poisoned some meat for him, had thoroughly envenomed a whole pound of hamburger, and early in the morning, before sunup, when he must have been near collapse with his hangover, he had stolen up to Mrs. Placer's house and put it by the kitchen door. He was so stealthy that Caesar never stirred in his fool's paradise there on the floor by Gran. We knew these to be the facts, for Mr. Murphy made no bones about them. Afterward, he had gone home and said a solemn Requiem for Shan-

JEAN STAFFORD

non in so loud a voice that someone sent for the police, and they took him away in the Black Maria to sober him up on strong green tea. By the time he was in the lockup and had confessed what he had done, it was far too late, for Caesar had already gulped down the meat. He suffered an undreamed-of agony in Gran's flower garden, and Daisy and I, unable to bear the sight of it, hiked up to the red rocks and shook there, wretchedly ripping to shreds the sand lilies that grew in the cracks. Flight was the only thing we could think of, but where could we go? We stared west at the mountains and quailed at the look of the stern white glacier; we wildly scanned the prairies for escape. "If only we were something besides kids! Besides girls!" mourned Daisy. I could not speak at all; I huddled in a niche of the rocks and cried.

No one in town, except, of course, her lodgers, had the slightest sympathy for Gran. The townsfolk allowed that Mr. Murphy was a drunk and was fighting Irish, but he had a heart and this was something that could never be said of Mrs. Placer. The neighbor who had called the police when he was chanting the "Dies Irae" before breakfast in that deafening monotone had said, "The poor guy is having some kind of a spell, so don't be rough on him, hear?" Mr. Murphy had become, in fact, a kind of hero; some people, stretching a point, said he was a saint for the way that every day and twice on Sunday he sang a memorial Mass over Shannon's grave, now marked with a chipped, cheap plaster figure of Saint Francis. He withdrew from the world more and more, seldom venturing into the streets at all, except when he went to the bootlegger

141

IN THE ZOO

to get a new bottle to snuggle into. All summer, all fall, we saw him as we passed by his yard, sitting at his dilapidated table, enfeebled with gin, graying, withering, turning his head ever and ever more slowly as he maneuvered the protocol of the kings and the queens and the knaves. Daisy and I could never stop to visit him again.

It went on like this, year after year. Daisy and I lived in a mesh of lies and evasions, baffled and mean, like rats in a maze. When we were old enough for beaux, we connived like sluts to see them, but we would never admit to their existence until Gran caught us out by some trick. Like this one, for example: Once, at the end of a long interrogation, she said to me, "I'm more relieved than I can tell you that you *don't* have anything to do with Jimmy Gilmore, because I happen to know that he is after only one thing in a girl," and then, off guard in the loving memory of sitting in the movies the night before with Jimmy, not even holding hands, I defended him and defeated myself, and Gran, smiling with success, said, "I *thought* you knew him. It's a pretty safe rule of thumb that where there's smoke there's fire." That finished Jimmy and me, for afterward I was nervous with him and I confounded and alarmed and finally bored him by trying to convince him, although the subject had not come up, that I did not doubt his good intentions.

Daisy and I would come home from school, or, later, from our jobs, with a small triumph or an interesting piece of news, and if we forgot ourselves and, in our exuberance, told Gran, we were hustled into court at once for cross-examination. Once, I remember, while I was still in high school, I told her about getting a part in a play. How very nice for me, she said, if that kind of make-believe seemed to me worth while. But what was my role? An old woman! A widow woman believed to be a witch? She did not care a red cent, but she did have to laugh in view of the fact that Miss Eccles, in charge of dramatics, had almost run her down in her car. And I would forgive her, would I not, if she did not come to see the play, and would not think her eccentric for not wanting to see herself ridiculed in public?

My pleasure strangled, I crawled, joy-killed, to our third-floor room. The room was small and its monstrous furniture was too big and the rag rugs were repulsive, but it was bright. We would not hang a blind at the window, and on this day I stood there staring into the mountains that burned with the sun. I feared the mountains, but at times like this their massiveness consoled me; they, at least, could not be gossiped about.

Why did we stay until we were grown? Daisy and I ask ourselves this question as we sit here on the bench in the municipal zoo, reminded of Mr. Murphy by the polar bear, reminded by the monkeys not of Shannon but of Mrs. Placer's insatiable gossips at their post-prandial feast.

"But how could we have left?" says Daisy, wringing her buttery hands. "It was the depression. We had no money. We had nowhere to go."

"All the same, we could have gone," I say, resentful still of the waste of all those years. "We could have come

IN THE ZOO

here and got jobs as waitresses. Or prostitutes, for that matter."

"I wouldn't have wanted to be a prostitute," says Daisy.

We agree that under the circumstances it would have been impossible for us to run away. The physical act would have been simple, for the city was not far and we could have stolen the bus fare or hitched a ride. Later, when we began to work as salesgirls in Kress's it would have been no trick at all to vanish one Saturday afternoon with our week's pay, without so much as going home to say good-bye. But it had been infinitely harder than that, for Gran, as we now see, held us trapped by our sense of guilt. We were vitiated, and we had no choice but to wait, flaccidly, for her to die.

You may be sure we did not unlearn those years as soon as we put her out of sight in the cemetery and sold her house for a song to the first boob who would buy it. Nor did we forget when we left the town for another one, where we had jobs at a dude camp——the town where Daisy now lives with a happy husband and two happy sons. The succubus did not relent for years, and I can still remember, in the beginning of our days at the Lazy S 3, overhearing an edgy millionaire say to his wife, naming my name, "That girl gives me the cold shivers. One would think she had just seen a murder." Well, I had. For years, whenever I woke in the night in fear or pain or loneliness, I would increase my suffering by the memory of Shannon, and my tears were as bitter as poor Mr. Murphy's.

We have never been back to Adams. But we see that house plainly, with the hopvines straggling over the

JEAN STAFFORD

porch. The windows are hung with the cheapest grade of marquisette, dipped into coffee to impart to it an unwilling color, neither white nor tan but individual and spitefully unattractive. We see the wicker rockers and the swing, and through the screen door we dimly make out the slightly veering corridor, along one wall of which stands a glass-doored bookcase; when we were children, it had contained not books but stale old cardboard boxes filled with such things as W.C.T.U. tracts and anti-cigarette literature and newspaper clippings related to sexual sin in the Christianized islands of the Pacific.

Even if we were able to close our minds' eyes to the past, Mr. Murphy would still be before us in the apotheosis of the polar bear. My pain becomes intolerable, and I am relieved when Daisy rescues us. "We've got to go," she says in a sudden panic. "I've got asthma coming on." We rush to the nearest exit of the city park and hail a cab, and, once inside it, Daisy gives herself an injection of adrenalin and then leans back. We are heartbroken and infuriated, and we cannot speak.

Two hours later, beside my train, we clutch each other as if we were drowning. We ought to go out to the nearest policeman and say, "We are not responsible women. You will have to take care of us because we cannot take care of ourselves." But gradually the storm begins to lull.

"You're sure you've got your ticket?" says Daisy. "You'll surely be able to get a roomette once you're on."

"I don't know about that," I say. "If there are any V.I.P.s on board, I won't have a chance. 'Spinsters and Orphans Last' is the motto of this line."

IN THE ZOO

Daisy smiles. "I didn't care," she says, "but I had to laugh when I saw that woman nab the redcap you had signalled to. I had a good notion to give her a piece of my mind."

"It will be a miracle if I ever see my bags again," I say, mounting the steps of the train. "Do you suppose that blackguardly porter knows about the twenty-dollar gold piece in my little suitcase?"

"Anything's possible!" cries Daisy, and begins to laugh. She is so pretty, standing there in her bright-red linen suit and her black velvet hat. A solitary ray of sunshine comes through a broken pane in the domed vault of the train shed and lies on her shoulder like a silver arrow.

"So long, Daisy!" I call as the train begins to move. She walks quickly along beside the train. "Watch out for pickpockets!" she calls.

"You too!" My voice is thin and lost in the increasing noise of the speeding train wheels. "Good-bye, old dear!"

I go at once to the club car and I appropriate the writing table, to the vexation of a harried priest, who snatches up the telegraph pad and gives me a sharp look. I write Daisy approximately the same letter I always write her under this particular set of circumstances, the burden of which is that nothing for either of us can ever be as bad as the past before Gran mercifully died. In a postscript I add: "There is a Roman Catholic priest (that is to say, he is *dressed* like one) sitting behind me although all the chairs on the opposite side of the car are empty. I can only conclude that he is looking over my shoulder, and while I do not want to cause you any alarm, I think you would be advised to be on the lookout for any appearance of miraculous medals, scapulars, papist booklets, etc., in the shops in your town. It really makes me laugh to see the way he is pretending that all he wants is for me to finish this letter so that he can have the table."

I sign my name and address the envelope, and I give up my place to the priest, who smiles nicely at me, and then I move across the car to watch the fields as they slip by. They are alfalfa fields, but you can bet your bottom dollar that they are chockablock with marijuana.

I begin to laugh. The fit is silent but it is devastating; it surges and rattles in my ribcage, and I turn my face to the window to avoid the narrow gaze of the Filipino bar boy. I must think of something sad to stop this unholy giggle, and I think of the polar bear. But even his bleak tragedy does not sober me. Wildly I fling open the newspaper I have brought and I pretend to be reading something screamingly funny. The words I see are in a Hollywood gossip column: "How a well-known starlet can get a divorce in Nevada without her crooner husband's consent, nobody knows. It won't be worth a plugged nickel here."

The Best of Everything

This story is an example of *third person narration*.

It is *realistic* in approach. The presentation is essentially *objective*—that is, the author supplies very little interpretation.

The *point of view* shifts from one major character to the other and then back again. First we see everything as Grace witnessed it—then as Ralph did—then, again, as Grace did.

The savage *tone* emerges more from the design of the plot and the incongruity of the characters forced together than from any devices of style. The *irony* arises from the events and is not particularly emphasized by the author's language.

There is a noteworthy *flashback* beginning on page 153.

The *climax* of the story occurs when Grace asks Ralph to stay with her.

The Best of Everything

by

RICHARD YATES

Nobody expected Grace to do any work the Friday before her wedding. In fact, nobody would let her, whether she wanted to or not.

A gardenia corsage lay in a cellophane box beside her typewriter—from Mr. Atwood, her boss—and tucked inside the envelope that came with it was a ten-dollar gift certificate from Bloomingdale's. Mr. Atwood had treated her with a special shy courtliness ever since the time she necked with him at the office Christmas party, and now when she went in to thank him he was all hunched over, rattling desk drawers, blushing and grinning and barely meeting her eyes.

"Aw, now, don't mention it, Grace," he said. "Pleasure's all mine. Here, you need a pin to put that gadget on with?"

"There's a pin that came with it," she said, holding up the corsage. "See? A nice white one."

Beaming, he watched her pin the flowers high on the lapel of her suit. Then he cleared his throat importantly and pulled out the writing panel of his desk, ready to give the morning's dictation. But it turned out there were only two short letters, and it wasn't until an hour later, when she caught him handing over a pile of Dictaphone cylinders to Central Typing, that she realized he had done her a favor.

"That's very sweet of you, Mr. Atwood," she said, "but I do think you ought to give me all your work today, just like any oth—"

"Aw, now, Grace," he said, "you only get married once."

The girls all made a fuss over her too, crowding around her desk and giggling, asking again and again to see Ralph's photograph ("Oh, he's *cute!*"), while the office manager looked on nervously, reluctant to be a spoilsport, but anxious to point out that it was, after all, a working day.

Then at lunch there was the traditional little party at Schrafft's—nine women and girls, giddy on their unfamiliar cocktails, letting their chicken à la king grow cold while they pummeled her with old times and good wishes. There were more flowers and another gift—a silver candy dish for which all the girls had whisperingly chipped in.

Grace said "Thank you" and "I certainly do appreciate it" and "I don't know what to say" until her head rang with the words and the corners of her mouth ached from smiling, and she thought the afternoon would never end.

Ralph called up about four o'clock, exuberant. "How ya doin', honey?" he asked, and before she could answer he said, "Listen. Guess what I got?"

THE BEST OF EVERYTHING

"I don't know. A present or something? What?" She tried to sound excited but it wasn't easy.

"A bonus. Fifty dollars." She could almost see the flattening of his lips as he said "fifty dollars" with the particular earnestness he reserved for pronouncing sums of money.

"Why, that's lovely, Ralph," she said, and if there was any tiredness in her voice he didn't notice it.

"Lovely, huh?" he said with a laugh, mocking the girlishness of the word. "Ya *like* that, huh Gracie? No, but I mean I was really surprised, ya know it? The boss siz, 'Here, Ralph,' and he hands me this envelope. He don't even crack a smile or nothin', and I'm wonderin', what's the deal here? I'm getting fired here, or what? He siz, 'G'ahead, Ralph, open it.' So I open it, and then I look at the boss and he's grinning a mile wide." He chuckled and sighed. "Well, so listen honey. What time ya want me to come over tonight?"

"Oh, I don't know. Soon as you can, I guess."

"Well listen. I gotta go over to Eddie's house and pick up that bag he's gonna loan me, so I might as well do that, go on home and eat, and then come over to your place around eight-thirty, nine o'clock. Okay?"

"All right," she said. "I'll see you then, darling." She had been calling him "darling" for only a short time— since it had become irrevocably clear that she was, after all, going to marry him—and the word still had an alien sound. As she straightened the stacks of stationery in her desk (because there was nothing else to do) a familiar little panic gripped her: She couldn't marry him—she hardly even *knew* him. Sometimes it occurred to her differently, that she couldn't marry him because she knew him too well, and either way it left her badly shaken, vulnerable to all the things that Martha, her roommate, had said from the very beginning.

"Isn't he funny?" Martha had said after their first date. "He says 'terlet.' I didn't know people really said 'terlet.'" And Grace had giggled, ready enough to agree that it *was* funny. That was a time when she had been ready to agree with Martha on practically anything—when it often seemed, in fact, that finding a girl like Martha from an ad in the *Times* was just about the luckiest thing that ever happened to her.

But Ralph had persisted all through the summer, and by fall she had begun standing up for him. "But what don't you *like* about him, Martha? He's perfectly nice."

"Oh, everybody's perfectly nice, Grace," Martha would say in her college voice, making perfectly nice a faintly absurd thing to be, and then she'd look up crossly from the careful painting of her fingernails. "It's just that he's such a little—a little *white worm*. Can't you see that?"

"Well, I certainly don't see what his *complexion* has to do with—"

"Oh, God, *you* know what I mean. Can't you see what I *mean?* Oh, and all those friends of his, his Eddie and his Marty and his George with their mean, ratty little clerks' lives and their mean, ratty little . . . It's just that they're all *alike*, those people. All they ever say is 'Hey, wha' happen t'ya Giants?' and 'Hey, wha' happen t'ya Yankees?' and they all live way out in some crowded little community, and their mothers have those damn little china elephants on the mantelpiece." And Martha

153

THE BEST OF EVERYTHING

would frown over her nail polish again, making it clear that the subject was closed.

All that fall and winter she was confused. For a while she tried going out only with Martha's kind of men—the kind that used words like "amusing" all the time and wore small-shouldered flannel suits like a uniform; and for a while she tried going out with no men at all. She even tried that crazy business with Mr. Atwood at the office Christmas party. And all the time Ralph kept calling up, hanging around, waiting for her to make up her mind. Once she took him home to meet her parents in Pennsylvania (where she never would have dreamed of taking Martha), but it wasn't until Easter time that she finally gave in.

They had gone to a dance somewhere in Queens, one of those big American Legion dances that Ralph's crowd was always going to, and when the band played "Easter Parade" he held her very close, hardly moving, and sang to her in a faint, whispering tenor. It was the kind of thing she'd never have expected Ralph to do—a sweet, gentle thing—and although it probably wasn't just then that she decided to marry him, it always seemed so afterwards.

That night she had told Martha, and she could still see the look on Martha's face. "Oh, Grace, you're not—surely you're not *serious*. I mean, I mean, I thought he was more or less of a *joke*—you can't really mean you want to—"

"Shut up! You just shut up, Martha!" And she'd cried all night. Even now she hated Martha for it; even as she stared blindly at a row of filing cabinets along the office wall, half sick with fear that Martha was right.

RICHARD YATES

The noise of giggles swept over her, and she saw with a start that two of the girls—Irene and Rose—were grinning over their typewriters and pointing at her. *"We* saw ya!" Irene sang. *"We* saw ya! Mooning again, huh Grace?" Then Rose did a burlesque of mooning, heaving her meager breasts and batting her eyes, and they both collapsed in laughter.

With an effort of will Grace resumed the guileless, open smile of a bride. The thing to do was concentrate on plans.

Tomorrow morning, "bright and early" as her mother would say, she would meet Ralph at Penn Station for the trip home. They'd arrive about one, and her parents would meet the train. "Good t'see ya, Ralph!" her father would say, and her mother would probably kiss him. A warm, homely love filled her; *they* wouldn't call him a white worm; *they* didn't have any ideas about Princeton men and "interesting" men and all the other kinds of men Martha was so stuck-up about. Then her father would probably take Ralph out for a beer and show him the paper mill where he worked (and at least Ralph wouldn't be snobby about a person working in a paper mill, either), and then Ralph's family and friends would come down from New York in the evening.

She'd have time for a long talk with her mother that night, and the next morning, "bright and early" (her eyes stung at the thought of her mother's plain, happy face), they would start getting dressed for the wedding. Then the church and the ceremony, and then the reception (Would her father get drunk? Would Muriel Ketchel sulk about not being a bridesmaid?), and finally the train to Atlantic City, and the hotel. But from the

THE BEST OF EVERYTHING

hotel on she couldn't plan any more. A door would lock behind her and there would be a wild, fantastic silence, and nobody else in all the world but Ralph to lead the way.

"Well, Grace," Mr. Atwood was saying, "I want to wish you every happiness." He was standing at her desk with his hat and coat on, and all around her was the chattering and scraping-back of chairs that meant it was five o'clock.

"Thank you, Mr. Atwood." She got to her feet, suddenly surrounded by all the girls in a bedlam of farewell.

"All the luck in the world, Grace."

"Drop us a card, huh, Grace? From Atlantic City?"

"So long, Grace."

"G'night, Grace, and listen: the best of everything."

Finally she was free of them all, out at the elevator, out of the building, hurrying through the crowds to the subway.

When she got home Martha was standing in the door of the kitchenette, looking very svelte in a crisp, new dress.

"Hi, Grace, I bet they ate you alive today, didn't they?"

"Oh, no," Grace said. "Everybody was—real nice." She sat down, exhausted, and dropped the flowers and the wrapped candy dish on a table. Then she noticed that the whole apartment was swept and dusted, and the dinner was cooking in the kitchenette. "Gee, everything looks wonderful," she said. "What'd you do all this for?"

"Oh, well, I got home early anyway," Martha said. Then she smiled, and it was one of the few times Grace had ever seen her look shy. "I just thought it might be nice to have the place looking decent for a change, when Ralph comes over."

"Well," Grace said, "it certainly was nice of you."

The way Martha looked now was even more surprising: she looked awkward. She was turning a greasy spatula in her fingers, holding it delicately away from her dress and examining it, as if she had something difficult to say. "Look, Grace," she began. "You do understand why I can't come to the wedding, don't you?"

"Oh, sure," Grace said, although in fact she didn't, exactly. It was something about having to go up to Harvard to see her brother before he went into the Army, but it had sounded like a lie from the beginning.

"It's just that I'd hate you to think I—well, anyway, I'm glad if you do understand. And the other thing I wanted to say is more important."

"What?"

"Well, just that I'm sorry for all the awful things that I used to say about Ralph. I never had a right to talk to you that way. He's a very sweet boy and I—well, I'm sorry, that's all."

It wasn't easy for Grace to hide a rush of gratitude and relief when she said, "Why, that's all right, Martha. I—"

"The chops are on fire!" Martha bolted for the kitchenette. "It's all right," she called back. "They're edible." And when she came out to serve dinner all her old composure was restored. "I'll have to eat and run," she

THE BEST OF EVERYTHING

said as they sat down. "My train leaves in forty minutes."

"But I thought you didn't have to go until *tomorrow!*"

"Well, I don't, actually," Martha said, "but I decided to go tonight. Because you see, Grace, another thing—if you can stand one more apology—another thing I'm sorry for is that I've hardly ever given you and Ralph a chance to be alone here. So tonight I'm going to clear out." She hesitated. "It'll be a sort of wedding gift from me, okay?" And then she smiled, not shyly this time but in a way that was more in character—the eyes subtly averted after a flicker of special meaning. It was a smile that Grace—through stages of suspicion, bewilderment, awe, and practiced imitation—had long ago come to associate with the word "sophisticated."

"Well, that's very sweet of you," Grace said, but she really didn't get the point just then. It wasn't until long after the meal was over and the dishes washed, until Martha had left for her train in a whirl of cosmetics and luggage and quick good-bys, that she began to understand.

She took a deep, voluptuous bath and spent a long time drying herself, posing in the mirror, filled with a strange, slow excitement. In her bedroom, from the rustling tissues of an expensive white box, she drew the prizes of her trousseau—a sheer nightgown of white nylon and a matching negligee—put them on, and went to the mirror again. She had never worn anything like this before, or felt like this, and the thought of letting Ralph see her like this sent her into the kitchenette for a glass of the special dry sherry Martha kept for cocktail parties. Then she turned out all the lights but one and, carrying her glass, went to the sofa and arranged herself there to wait for him. After a while she got up and brought the sherry bottle over to the coffee table, where she set it on a tray with another glass.

When Ralph left the office he felt vaguely let down. Somehow, he'd expected more of the Friday before his wedding. The bonus check had been all right (though secretly he'd been counting on twice that amount), and the boys had bought him a drink at lunch and kidded around in the appropriate way ("Ah, don't feel too bad, Ralph—worse things could happen"), but still, there ought to have been a real party. Not just the boys in the office, but Eddie, and *all* his friends. Instead there would only be meeting Eddie at the White Rose like every other night of the year, and riding home to borrow Eddie's suitcase and to eat, and then having to ride all the way back to Manhattan just to see Grace for an hour or two. Eddie wasn't in the bar when he arrived, which sharpened the edge of his loneliness. Morosely he drank a beer, waiting.

Eddie was his best friend and an ideal Best Man because he'd been in on the courtship of Grace from the start. It was in this very bar, in fact, that Ralph had told him about their first date last summer: "Ooh, Eddie— what a figger!"

And Eddie had grinned. "Yeah? So what's the roommate like?"

"Ah, you don't want the roommate, Eddie. The roommate's a dog. A snob, too, I think. No, but this *other* one, this little *Gracie*—boy, I mean, she is *stacked*."

THE BEST OF EVERYTHING

Half the fun of every date—even more than half—had been telling Eddie about it afterwards, exaggerating a little here and there, asking Eddie's advice on tactics. But after today, like so many other pleasures, it would all be left behind. Gracie had promised him at least one night off a week to spend with the boys, after they were married, but even so it would never be the same. Girls never understood a thing like friendship.

There was a ball game on the bar's television screen and he watched it idly, his throat swelling in a sentimental pain of loss. Nearly all his life had been devoted to the friendship of boys and men, to trying to be a good guy, and now the best of it was over.

Finally Eddie's stiff finger jabbed the seat of his pants in greeting. "Whaddya say, sport?"

Ralph narrowed his eyes to indolent contempt, and slowly turned around. "Wha' happen ta you, wise guy? Get lost?"

"Whaddya—in a hurry a somethin'?" Eddie barely moved his lips when he spoke. "Can't wait two minutes?" He slouched on a stool and slid a quarter at the bartender. "Draw one, there, Jack."

They drank in silence for a while, staring at the television. "Got a little bonus today," Ralph said. "Fifty dollars."

"Yeah?" Eddie said. "Good."

A batter struck out; the inning was over and the commercial came on. "So?" Eddie said, rocking the beer around in his glass. "Still gonna get married?"

"Why not?" Ralph said with a shrug. "Listen, finish that, willya? I wanna get a move on."

"Wait awhile, wait awhile. What's ya hurry?"

RICHARD YATES

"C'mon, willya?" Ralph stepped impatiently away from the bar. "I wanna go pick up ya bag."

"Ah, bag schmagg."

Ralph moved up close again and glowered at him. "Look, wise guy. Nobody's gonna *make* ya loan me the goddam bag, ya know. I don't wanna break ya *heart* or nothin'—"

"Arright, arright, arright. You'll getcha bag. Don't worry so much." He finished the beer and wiped his mouth. "Let's go."

Having to borrow a bag for his wedding trip was a sore point with Ralph; he'd much rather have bought one of his own. There was a fine one displayed in the window of a luggage shop they passed every night on their way to the subway—a big, tawny Gladstone with a zippered compartment on the side, at thirty-nine ninety-five—and Ralph had had his eye on it ever since Easter time. "Think I'll buy that," he'd told Eddie, in the same offhand way that a day or so before he had announced his engagement ("Think I'll marry the girl"). Eddie's response to both remarks had been the same: "Whaddya—crazy?" Both times Ralph had said, "Why not?" and in defense of the bag he had added, "Gonna get married, I'll *need* somethin' like that." From then on it was as if the bag, almost as much as Gracie herself, had become the symbol of the new and richer life he sought. But after the ring and the new clothes and all the other expenses, he'd found at last that he couldn't afford it; he had settled for the loan of Eddie's which was similar but cheaper and worn, and without the zippered compartment.

THE BEST OF EVERYTHING

Now as they passed the luggage shop he stopped, caught in the grip of a reckless idea. "Hey wait awhile, Eddie. Know what I think I'll do with that fifty-dollar bonus? I think I'll buy that bag right now." He felt breathless.

"Whaddya—*crazy?* Forty bucks for a bag you'll use maybe one time a year? Ya crazy, Ralph. C'mon."

"Ah—I dunno. Ya think so?"

"Listen, you better *keep* ya money, boy. You're gonna *need* it."

"Ah—yeah," Ralph said at last. "I guess ya right." And he fell in step with Eddie again, heading for the subway. This was the way things usually turned out in his life; he could never own a bag like that until he made a better salary, and he accepted it—just as he'd accepted without question, after the first thin sigh, the knowledge that he'd never possess his bride until after the wedding.

The subway swallowed them, rattled and banged them along in a rocking, mindless trance for half an hour, and disgorged them at last into the cool early evening of Queens.

Removing their coats and loosening their ties, they let the breeze dry their sweated shirts as they walked. "So what's the deal?" Eddie asked. "What time we supposed to show up in this Pennsylvania burg tomorra?"

"Ah, suit yourself," Ralph said. "Any time in the evening's okay."

"So whadda we do then? What the hell can ya *do* in a hillbilly town like that, anyway?"

"Ah, I dunno," Ralph said defensively. "Sit around

and talk, I guess; drink beer with Gracie's old man or somethin'."

"Some week end," Eddie said. "Big, big deal."

Ralph stopped on the sidewalk, suddenly enraged, his damp coat wadded in his fist. "Look, you bastid. Nobody's gonna *make* ya come, ya know—you or Marty or George or any a the rest of 'em. Get that straight. You're not doin' *me* no favors, unnastand?"

"Whatsa matta?" Eddie inquired. "Whatsa matta? Can'tcha take a joke?"

"Joke," Ralph said. "You're fulla jokes." And plodding sullenly in Eddie's wake he felt close to tears.

They turned off into the block where they both lived, a double row of neat, identical houses, bordering the street where they'd fought and loafed and played stickball all their lives. Eddie pushed open the front door of his house and ushered Ralph into the vestibule, with its homely smell of cauliflower and overshoes. "G'wan in," he said, jerking a thumb at the closed living-room door, and he hung back to let Ralph go first.

Ralph opened the door and took three steps inside it before it hit him like a sock on the jaw. The room, dead silent, was packed deep with grinning, red-faced men—Marty, George, the boys from the block, the boys from the office—everybody, all his friends, all on their feet and poised motionless in a solid mass. Skinny Maguire was crouched at the upright piano, his spread fingers high over the keys, and when he struck the first rollicking chords they all roared into song, beating time with their fists, their enormous grins distorting the words:

THE BEST OF EVERYTHING

"Fa he's a jally guh fella
Fa he's a jally guh fella
Fa he's a jally guh fell-ah
That nobody can deny!"

Weakly Ralph retreated a step on the carpet and stood there wide-eyed, swallowing, holding his coat. "That nobody can deny!" they sang, "That nobody can deny!" And as they swung into the second chorus Eddie's father appeared through the dining-room curtains, bald and beaming, in full song, with a great glass pitcher of beer in either hand. At last Skinny hammered out the final line:

"That—no—bod—dee—can—dee—nye!"

And they all surged forward cheering, grabbing Ralph's hand, pounding his arms and his back while he stood trembling, his own voice lost under the noise. "Gee, fellas—thanks. I—I don't know what to—thanks, fellas. . . ."

Then the crowd cleaved in half, and Eddie made his way slowly down the middle. His eyes gleamed in a smile of love, and from his bashful hand the suitcase—not his own, but a new one: the big, tawny Gladstone with the zippered compartment on the side.

"Speech!" they were yelling. *"Speech! Speech!"*

But Ralph couldn't speak and couldn't smile. He could hardly even see.

At ten o'clock Grace began walking around the apartment and biting her lip. What if he wasn't coming? But of course he was coming. She sat down again and carefully smoothed the billows of nylon around her thighs, forcing herself to be calm. The whole thing would be ruined if she was nervous.

The noise of the doorbell was like an electric shock. She was halfway to the door before she stopped, breathing hard, and composed herself again. Then she pressed the buzzer and opened the door a crack to watch for him on the stairs.

When she saw he was carrying a suitcase, and saw the pale seriousness of his face as he mounted the stairs, she thought at first that he knew; he had come prepared to lock the door and take her in his arms. "Hello, darling," she said softly, and opened the door wider.

"Hi, baby." He brushed past her and walked inside. "Guess I'm late, huh? You in bed?"

"No." She closed the door and leaned against it with both hands holding the doorknob at the small of her back, the way heroines close doors in the movies. "I was just—waiting for you."

He wasn't looking at her. He went to the sofa and sat down, holding the suitcase on his lap and running his fingers over its surface. "Gracie," he said, barely above a whisper. "Look at this."

She looked at it, and then into his tragic eyes.

"Remember," he said, "I told you about that bag I wanted to buy? Forty dollars?" He stopped and looked around. "Hey, where's Martha? She in bed?"

"She's gone, darling," Grace said, moving slowly toward the sofa. "She's gone for the whole week end." She sat down beside him, leaned close and gave him Martha's special smile.

THE BEST OF EVERYTHING

"Oh yeah?" he said. "Well anyway, listen. I said I was gonna borrow Eddie's bag instead, remember?"

"Yes."

"Well, so tonight at the White Rose I siz, 'C'mon, Eddie, let's go home pick up ya bag.' He siz, 'Ah, bag schmagg.' I siz, 'Whatsa matta?' but he don't say nothin', see? So we go home to his place and the living room door's shut, see?"

She squirmed closer and put her head on his chest. Automatically he raised an arm and dropped it around her shoulders, still talking. "He siz, 'G'head, Ralph, open the door.' I siz, 'Whatsa deal?' He siz, 'Never mind, Ralph, open the door.' So I open the door, and oh Jesus." His fingers gripped her shoulder with such intensity that she looked up at him in alarm.

"They was all there, Gracie," he said. "All the fellas. Playin' the piana, singin', cheerin'—" His voice wavered and his eyelids fluttered shut, their lashes wet. "A big surprise party," he said, trying to smile. "Fa me. Can ya beat that, Gracie? And then—and then Eddie comes out and—Eddie comes out and hands me this. The very same bag I been looking at all this time. He bought it with his own money and he didn't say nothin', just to give me a surprise. 'Here, Ralph,' he siz. 'Just to let ya know you're the greatest guy in the world.' " His fingers tightened again, trembling. "I cried, Gracie," he whispered. "I couldn't help it. I don't think the fellas saw it or anything, but I was cryin'." He turned his face away and worked his lips in a tremendous effort to hold back the tears.

"Would you like a drink, darling?" she asked tenderly.

"Nah, that's all right, Gracie. I'm all right." Gently

he set the suitcase on the carpet. "Only, gimme a cigarette, huh?"

She got one from the coffee table, put it in his lips and lit it. "Let me get you a drink," she urged.

He frowned through the smoke. "Whaddya got, that sherry wine? Nah, I don't like that stuff. Anyway, I'm fulla beer." He leaned back and closed his eyes. "And then Eddie's mother feeds us this terrific meal," he went on, and his voice was almost normal now. "We had *steaks;* we had French-fried *potatas,*" his head rolled on the sofa-back with each item, "lettuce-and-tomato *salad, pickles, bread, butter*—everything. The works."

"Well," she said. "Wasn't that nice?"

"And afterwards we had ice cream and coffee," he said, "and all the beer we could drink. It was a real spread."

Grace ran her hands over her lap, partly to smooth the nylon and partly to dry the moisture on her palms. "Well, that was certainly nice of them," she said. They sat there silent for what seemed a long time.

"I can only stay a minute, Gracie," Ralph said at last. "I promised 'em I'd be back."

Her heart thumped under the nylon. "Ralph, do you —do you like this?"

"What, honey?"

"My negligee. You weren't supposed to see it until— after the wedding, but I thought I'd—"

"Nice," he said, feeling the flimsy material between thumb and index finger, like a merchant. "Very nice. Wudga pay fa this, honey?"

"Oh—I don't know. But do you like it?"

He kissed her and began, at last, to stroke her with his

167

THE BEST OF EVERYTHING

hands. "Nice," he kept saying. "Nice. Hey, I like this." His hand hesitated at the low neckline, then slipped inside.

"I do love you, Ralph," she whispered. "You know that, don't you?"

His fingers pinched her breast, once, and slid quickly out again. The policy of restraint, the habit of months was too strong to break. "Sure," he said. "And I love you, baby. Now, you be a good girl and get ya beauty sleep, and I'll see ya in the morning. Okay?"

"Oh, Ralph. Don't go. Stay."

"Ah, I promised the fellas, Gracie." He stood up and straightened his clothes. "They're waitin' fa me, out to Eddie's."

She blazed to her feet, but the cry that was meant for a woman's appeal came out, through her tightening lips, as the whine of a wife. "Can't they wait?"

"Whaddya—*crazy?*" He backed away, eyes round with righteousness. She would *have* to understand. If this was the way she acted *before* the wedding, how the hell was it going to be *afterwards?* "Have a *heart,* willya? Keep the fellas waitin' *tonight?* After all they done *fa me?*"

After a second or two, during which her face became less pretty than he had ever seen it before, she was able to smile. "Of course not, darling. You're right."

He came forward again and gently brushed the tip of her chin with his fist, a husband reassured. " 'At's more like it," he said. "So I'll see ya, Penn Station, nine o'clock tomorra. Right, Gracie? Only, before I go—" He winked and slapped his belly. "I'm fulla beer. Mind if I use ya terlet?"

RICHARD YATES

When he came out of the bathroom she was waiting to say good-night, standing with her arms folded across her chest, as if for warmth. Lovingly he hefted the new suitcase and joined her at the door. "Okay, then, baby," he said, and kissed her. "Nine o'clock. Don't forget, now."

She smiled tiredly and opened the door for him. "Don't worry, Ralph," she said. "I'll be there."

The Yellow Raft

Third person narration. The story represents a special variety of *realism,* for which I will not attempt to invent a fancy title or epithet. You should note, however, that there is an effect of non-human innocence about the antics of the planes and the pilot in the raft. That is, while the substance of the story seems real and not even particularly unusual, the observation is most strange. It is this adaptation of ordinary realism that gives the story its *tone* of horror and pity.

At only one point and then only for a few sentences do we see things from the *point of view* of the one human actor in the story. Technically speaking, it is told mostly from an unidentified viewpoint, but it is as if the author had assumed the impersonality of the ocean itself and were telling all this as the ocean saw it.

Note the abundance of *concrete visual images.* Note how the occasional similes point up some of the ironies of modern war.

The Yellow Raft

by

EVAN S. CONNELL, JR.

From the direction of the Solomon Islands came a damaged Navy fighter, high in the air, but gliding steadily down upon the ocean. The broad paddle blades of the propeller revolved uselessly with a dull whirring noise, turned only by the wind. Far below, quite small but growing larger, raced the shadow of the descending fighter. Presently they were very close together, the aircraft and its shadow, but each time they seemed about to merge they broke apart—the long fuselage tilting farther backward, raising the cold heavy engine for another moment, while the shadow, like some distraught creature, leaped hastily through the whitecaps. Finally the engine plunged into a wave. The fuselage stood briefly erect, a strange blue buoy riddled by gunfire, and then, bubbling, inclining, it sank beneath the greasy water. A few seconds later, as if propelled by a spring, a small yellow raft hurtled to the surface with such violence that it almost took off. It wallowed back and forth, the sides lapped with oil. Suddenly a bloody

EVAN S. CONNELL, JR.

human hand rose out of the ocean and clutched it. For a little while nothing else happened; the raft floated calmly over the swells and the man held on. Then he dragged himself into the raft and lay there crying bitterly. A few minutes later he was sitting up, cross-legged, balancing himself against the motion of the raft and squinting toward the southern horizon, for it was in that direction he had been flying and from that direction help would come. After staring at the horizon for about an hour he pulled off his helmet and began toying with the radio cord; then he lay down in the bottom of the raft and covered his face with his hands. Late that afternoon he again sat up and began to open the pouches along the inside walls of his raft. He found signal flares, first-aid equipment, some dehydrated rations, and a few luxuries, and when the sun went down he had just finished eating some candy and was lighting a cigarette. He blew a few smoke rings in defiance of the sea, however a west wind developed and before long he stopped mocking his host; he zipped up his green coveralls to the neck and turned up the collar against the spray. Next he tightened the straps and drawstrings of his life jacket and lay down once more, bracing his hands and feet against the sides. He was sick at his stomach and his wounds were bleeding again. Stars appeared all around the raft. Several hours passed in total silence, except for the slosh of water and the occasional squeak of rubber as the raft bent over the crest of a wave. Spume broke lightly but persistently on the man huddling with his back to the wind. Suddenly a rocket whistled up from the raft and illuminated the scene. No sooner had its light died away than an-

THE YELLOW RAFT

other rocket burst, and then another, and another, and another until there were no more. But there was no answer. Overhead wheeled the Southern Cross, Corvus, Hydra, and Libra. Before dawn the lost pilot was crouching on hands and knees, peering intently toward the southern horizon. Presently he thought he saw a marine reptile as large as a whale, but with a long swanlike neck, pass underneath the raft and emerge from the water some distance away, and as he looked into the depths the pilot discovered that the sea was filled with living things. The water bulged all around and from everywhere bloomed the fiery tentacles of the sun. Occasionally, on a crest, the pilot was drenched with spray. Then he waited with a remote stare as the raft, with a sickening, twisting slide, sank into the trough where the ocean and the ragged scud seemed about to close over it. A flashlight on the bottom of the raft rolled to one side, hesitated, and came rolling rapidly back, while a deepening puddle of sea water appeared now at the pilot's feet and now at his head and sometimes submerged the flashlight. The rubber walls of the raft were slippery, and the pouches from which he had taken the rockets and the cigarettes were now brimming with water. The drawstrings of his life jacket slapped wildly back and forth. He had put on his canvas helmet again, and a pair of thin leather gloves to protect himself from the sting of the spray. Stubby, foaming waves rose abruptly, without rhythm, to sweep over the walls of the raft, and left the pilot covered with salty bubbles. The ocean and the sky had fused; he could not tell whether he was vertical or horizontal, and he no longer cared. By noon he was drifting through a

EVAN S. CONNELL, JR.

steady rain, his eyes closed. Whenever the raft slipped into a trough the final vestige of light disappeared; then, with a splash and the squeak of taut rubber, it spun up the side of the next wave, met the onrushing crest, and whirled down again into darkness. In the middle of that afternoon a layer of dingy phosphorescent light disjoined the sea from the sky; then the waves grew massive and took on a solid greenish-black hue, like volcanic glass, each vast undersurface curved and scratched as if by the grinding of pebbles. The pilot waited and watched as one colossal wave after another dove under the bounding yellow raft. When the storm had passed it was night again and the constellations were overhead as before.

At dawn, from the south, came a Catalina flying boat, a plump and graceless creation known as the PBY— phlegmatic in the air, more at home resting its deep snowy breast in the water. It approached, high and slow, and almost flew beyond the raft. But finally the tremendous wing of the PBY inclined slightly toward a yellow dot on the ocean, and in a stately spiral the flying boat descended, keeping the raft always within its orbit. Several minutes later, a few yards above the water, the PBY skimmed by the raft. Except for the flashlight rolling idly back and forth and glittering in the sunshine, the yellow raft was empty. The PBY climbed a few hundred feet, and, after turning, crossed over the raft again. Then it climbed a little more and began to circle the raft. All morning long the Catalina circled, holding its breast high like a great blue heron in flight, the gun barrels, propellers, and plexiglass blisters reflecting the tropical sun. For a while at the

THE YELLOW RAFT

beginning of the search it flew tightly around the raft, low enough to touch the water in a few seconds, but later on it climbed to an altitude from which the raft looked like a toy on a pond. There was nothing else in sight. The only shadow on the sea was that of the Navy flying boat moving in slow, monotonous circles around and around the deserted rubber raft. At one time the PBY angled upward nearly a mile, its twin engines buzzing like flies in a vacant room, but after a few minutes it came spiraling down to continue as before, the inner wing pointing so steadily at the gaudy raft that the two objects might have been connected by a wire. The horizon remained empty. On the tranquil, sunny ocean no spars or crushed debris were floating, nothing to mark the place where the fighter had gone down, just the raft which was smeared with oil and flecked with salt foam. Early that afternoon a blister slid open near the tail of the Catalina, and a moment later a cluster of empty beer cans fell like little bombs in a smooth glittering trajectory toward the sea, splashed, and began filling with water. A few waxed sandwich papers came fluttering down and floated on the ocean some distance ahead of the sinking beer cans. All through the long afternoon nothing else happened, except that once again the water seemed to grow restless, and a thin veil materialized in the sky, diminishing the light of the sun and deadening the rich color of the Coral Sea. Well before dark the Catalina turned inward, carefully, till it pointed straight at the raft. Then for the first time in many hours the insignia on its prow—a belligerent little duck with a bomb and a pair of binoculars—rode vertically over the waves.

EVAN S. CONNELL, JR.

The prow of the Catalina dropped as it approached the raft, and the tenor of its engines began to rise. The huge flying boat descended with ponderous dignity, as a dowager might stoop to retrieve a lost glove, and with a low, hoarse scream it passed directly over the raft. An instant later, inside the blue-black hull, a long thin gun began to rattle. The raft bounced on the water until the gunfire ceased. The strange dance ended. The yellow raft fell back, torn into fragments of cork and loose, deflated rubber. From these remains came floating an iridescent dye, as green as a rainbow. The Catalina, its work complete, began to rise. Higher and higher in the air, never changing course, it flew majestically toward the infinite horizon, leaving the darkness and the silence.

THE

CONCEPTS

of

FICTION

5

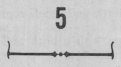

Unity

We learn an inestimable amount about how to write
from our reading. By emulating models we can learn
many devices for unifying our own material. Later in this
chapter I will enumerate some of the principal devices
and examine them at greater length in the following
chapters of this section.

But there remains much that we cannot learn from
anyone else. And one overwhelming challenge haunts every
honest writer every time he begins a new story. *How
shall he conceive the unity of his work?*

This may seem like a minor or elusive problem. For the
critic or the general reader it may be so. For the writer
it may be elusive—maddeningly so—but it will not be
minor. He knows that conceiving an over-all unity is just
about the same as determining for what ends he will use
the fictional devices at his command. It is the conception
that tells him what to include, what to leave out, where
to start, and when to round out his conclusion. It must
guide him in the selection and manipulation of all the elements of fiction from which he hopes to fashion a story.

If one were content merely to imitate a story already
in print there would be no problem. But we want to—in

the final analysis we have to—imitate life. And life, un happily, provides far more examples of confusion an multiplicity than of unity.

Probably only birth and death represent any clear-c terminals in actual life—and it is unthinkable that a stories should begin with a birth and end with a deat Furthermore, consistency in life is almost accidental. Th thoughts and emotions of ten o'clock in the morning a almost certain to be followed by distractions at eleve Insignificant distractions? Not at all. When we think abo the matter honestly, we realize that no distraction is i significant. In life everything is influenced by everythir else. There are no neat, persistent patterns in the surfa of life. If there were they would not stand still so we cou copy them.

Life is a constant flux, and even one man's experien is full of chaotic diversions, inconclusive fadings away, an reappearances that seem more like new beginnings th ends.

In a lot of fiction, the conflicts of courtship end with marriage. The courtship is given an appearance of uni by such a termination. The object that was sought co sistently through courtship has been achieved. Why n end one's own story where many stories have ended?

Why not? Because the honestly troubled writer, fu bling for his own conception of a story that will imita life, remembers that life didn't pause for the flicker an eyelash when the bride said, "I do." Life stumbl and surged on, carrying away or rearranging all artific boundaries. Before there is time to write of it, the ma riage that seemed to mark the end of an epoch seems ev more emphatically to mark the beginning of another— to be merely another event in an endless sequence events.

I am not trying to raise a philosophical quibble emphasizing this discrepancy between unbounded life a the unity required in fiction. I am talking about somethi we are obliged to feel with a kind of desperation each time we begin to transpose experience into fiction.

The writer possesses, or is possessed by, deeply understood experience. He knows he has "something to say." He has some technical abilities to say it. But what—exactly what—is "it"? Ah, if life only presented itself to us in neatly measured chunks, each one wrapped and sealed so there would be no blending of one sort of experience with another. . . .

He is tempted to shout at all the mocking powers of the universe that you cannot imitate the formlessness of life by giving it any form at all.

Yet he knows he has to make certain tentative decisions about where to begin and end—from which side and level to cut into his material—if he is going to write at all. In one fashion or another he has to say, "Once upon a time. . . ." And this arbitrary declaration (which means "what I have to tell you began exactly *here*") must be followed by a statement of the situation prevailing when *"it all began."* He has to begin to *impose* unity on raw material that has none.

It is in choosing how to impose unity that a writer declares or surrenders his independence. Here he chooses to follow a formula—which might have been very good for someone else's story—or invent a form that will be truly responsible to the still shapeless material that is his alone. The way in which he will impose unity on disorder determines whether his work will be really an imitation of life or not.

If he chooses independence (rather than formula) he still cannot begin his imposition of unifying devices nor his selection of material to imitate life as it appears to him when he contemplates it disinterestedly. He must start by imitating it as it appears when it is focused by emotion. So if he cares and cares deeply about his subject he has an initial advantage. Though life may appear an endless

205

flux to the speculative mind, an emotional involvement makes it appear unified around (before and after) a momentary crisis.

The writer of an original story begins to shape his material by accepting an emotional commitment to it—very much as if he himself were the first character to appear in the story to be. This primary commitment is usually no more than scaffolding. It will be totally replaced by structural elements of the story itself before the story is done. But it offers an initial base for selecting one sort of character rather than another to play the principal role, for selecting one kind of conflict rather than another to demonstrate what truly was in issue, and for selecting a central action or plot to show what values triumphed and what ones lost as the conflict progressed.

Pure experience asks, What do I mean? The writer's first answer is, You mean what I *want* you to mean. So give me *this* character, *that* situation, and *those* possibilities of action to start with—no others please—and I will show everyone what you meant to me.

This passionate wish to *make* experience yield particular meaning is the heart of the creative act, the initial selection from which subsequent choices flow with an increasingly rational justification. The finishing touches on a story, the final impositions of unity, may be made as coldly, logically, conventionally as you wish. The first choices to cut into experience must be irrational and emotional—just exactly *as if* you were a character in your story, preferring one thing to another simply because you are yourself and want what you want out of a bewildering world.

This is the way the creative act of writing a story begins, but I have not meant to imply that one must complete a self-conscious and exhaustive examination of his soul before he begins each story. The primary choice of a way to segment experience is no doubt generally made by habit

It is one's second nature to admit some ready-made unities in experience and to accept them unquestioningly. One says automatically—if not quite correctly—"Oh, I know where the conflict began for the people I mean to write about. I'll start at that beginning." That's fine when it works. It's an example, perhaps, of the author unconsciously playing a character, exercising his prejudices to give a preliminary unity to his material.

And of course there are some subjects in which a natural unity is more readily apparent than in others. If your subject is to be the visit of a mysterious stranger, then what is more simple than to begin the story with his arrival and conclude it with his departure? The unity of many fine stories seems to have been given the author by those unifying labels we use in ordinary life: a visit, a love affair, a contest, a disaster, a journey, or a celebration.

Any writer with good common sense will respect these "given" unities when he can. I have not been probing the mysteries of how a writer begins to unify his work with the intent of recommending something fancy and profound instead of what is candid and easy.

Whenever there is an easy way to do something—and do it right—by all means prefer the easy way. Heaven knows, there are enough infinitely difficult things about writing so that one deserves any free throws he gets.

Yet never forget that this matter of discovering the appropriate unities for your material—and it is a question of discovery—is a very large part of the art of fiction.

Look at a story as brief and, at first glance, as simple as "The Yellow Raft" and tell me, if you can, what there is in the nature of the subject matter that dictates opening the story where it opens and ending it where it ends.

Basically the opening situation we are given is this: A fighter plane has been damaged and is trying to limp home.

(Why aren't we told where and how it was damaged? Where it came from originally? Where the pilot came from? And so on.)

The plane doesn't make it. It falls in the water. Finis. The End.

But this is not the end of Mr. Connell's story.

Ah. Yes. Well, the pilot wasn't killed immediately. He manages to free himself and get aboard the raft. Presently he dies. Finis. The End.

Not yet. Mr. Connell does not stop there.

Ah. A patrol plane comes searching for the downed flier. Circles. Shoots up the raft. Now the ocean is empty again. Finis. The End. At exactly the moment *this* story should end.

When we read Mr. Connell's little story critically we can discern the way he has built unities into it. Perhaps foremost there is a unity of tone, of bleak, inhuman emptiness mocking the fall of a human venture. There is a unity of language. There is a unity of action (imposed by the author's conception, I think, rather than dictated by any common assumption of what constitutes a unified action).

Look at almost any of the stories in this book and you will find them very skillfully unified. But only in "That Lovely Green Boat" perhaps is there anything in the nature of the material that gives us readers any very easy indication of why the particular unities were chosen. There we have the story of a summer in the lives of three adolescents who prize a green duck boat. The content of the story is naturally about what they do with the boat (and what it represents). The story ends naturally when the boat is destroyed.

The story tells itself the way the author has told it.

But I defy you to demonstrate that the same is true of any of the other stories. We must say of each of them that the unities were developed rather than exploited, that they are a product of the author's brooding over his sub-ject matter rather than his good fortune in "having an experience worth telling about."

In each there is a mystery in the way the author has built a form that satisfies our need for unity without violat-ing our feeling that life is a shapeless flux. And it is just that mystery which the writer needs to explore.

A sophisticated and complex story like "In the Zoo" confronts us squarely with this mystery. The present scene —a visit between two sisters—would seem to have a kind of natural unity, except there is no obvious link between this present scene and the action of the past that forms the main body of the story. Yes, the sisters *remember* the past while they sit together in the zoo. Couldn't they have done so somewhere else? Alone? Is the present scene of the visit a mere tribute the author has paid to the fact that life is chaotic in its circumstances?

Not at all. And perhaps by showing the way the author has built—or discovered—the unifying lines between past and present, we may get a helpful notion of how a writer must work after he has unified his conception and made a beginning.

But in pointing out the unity that does exist in the story, we must not lose sight of the fractured—almost chaotic—surface of time and place that the author has mastered. *That* seems as inconsecutive as memory itself.

For that matter, the action of the past is not one simple, naturally unified chunk. To be sure, there is the episode (written in scenic form) in which the two little girls ac-company Mr. Murphy on his ill-fated crusade against Mrs. Placer. But this episode is only a part of a past action that persists for years from an indefinite beginning to no dramatic resolution at all. (The action is, for the most part, given by means of narrative and half-scene.)

Instead of limiting her story to whatever natural unities are present in the conflict between Murphy and Mrs.

Placer, the author has daringly expanded the scope until it seems to include nothing less than the entire lives of the two sisters.

But, having noted this apparently reckless expansion in certain aspects, we are ready to define the one firm principle of unity that substitutes for those disregarded.

It is the establishment of one—and only one—pattern in the lives of the sisters that is the beautifully expanded, beautifully limited subject of the story. How did Mrs. Placer first outrage her innocent victims and then reproduce in them the very self-righteousness which they had hated and from which they had suffered? In giving unity to this story, the author must have used this question to determine what that unity could include. Anything that answered the question was part of her story. Anything that did not—however much it might have told us about the lives of the sisters in other respects—should not have been included.

But beyond any such rationalized explanations of how the story was unified, we have to conclude that what Miss Stafford wanted her material to mean directed the choice of devices. What she wanted it to mean is revealed as the theme of the story: Victims may take on the likeness of their persecutor. In the ultimate, thematic declaration of a fully realized piece of fiction we see the clearest reflection of the personal will from which the form emerged. The end of writing reveals the beginning. Looking backward, we may say that it was the not-yet-articulated theme which "realized itself" by pruning away the irrelevancies that may, in the process of composition, have risen in the author's imagination.

Does that sound like magic? Well, of course it is. She only knew what she meant to say when she had made her story say it, but . . . she knew from the beginning what she meant. Yes, that's the way it works in writing fiction. That's the magic of it. No examination of technique can fully explain it.

Still we'll go on examining techniques, for without them the magic could not be accomplished. The circle of the imagination could never be closed.

Bringing a story along the way from a first conception to completed form has often struck me as an ungainly progress. First the chosen material dictates. Among other things, it dictates certain unities which the writer is well-advised to accept.

Then comes the point at which the writer must dictate to his material.

The writer is pushed, then he pulls. The material regains its momentum. It pushes again. The writer pulls again. This makes for progress toward a good story—when the writer and the material move in the same direction. So it's up to the writer to keep his eyes open and his mind nimble when he takes his turn at supplying momentum, for the material is blind and incapable of making alternate choices. It is incapable of reinforcing unities when the inherent ones prove insufficient.

One may at least conjecture that the choice of an opening for "In the Zoo" was a highly rationalized one and that it was made for the sake of further unifying the story. True enough, we are told that the "poor blind bear" reminds one of the sisters of Mr. Murphy. So in whatever pity we feel for the dumb, caged creature, we are being prepared to spend our pity on Mr. Murphy as soon as we begin to understand that he might also be considered a dumb, caged creature. The bear is a symbol of a particular sort of suffering, a preparatory symbol, quite appropriately placed at the beginning of this story to stand as a sign for what will presently be shown in realistic, non-symbolic terms.

As the author presents him—and probably conceived him in the first place—he is a natural enough symbol. Anyone, we think, might have seen the similarity between him and Murphy, and in pitying one, pity the other.

The bear functions in another way, enforcing another unity upon the material of the story from the very beginning. Since this is to be a story in which animals play an important part, what happens to the dog Laddy after his name is changed to Caesar is at the very heart of the story's meaning. The wanton killing of the monkey Shannon is the high moment of such dramatic and overt action as the story contains. Shannon and Caesar are not symbolic animals, except secondarily. Primarily they are the dumb, living creatures who become agents of the grotesque and warring passions of their masters. They have a concrete and irreplaceable role in the action. Therefore, what could be more appropriate, more subtly and shrewdly conceived by the author, than to begin telling the story by focusing the reader's attention and emotion on another such animal?

In the opening scene we know that this bear is only a bear and that whatever emotion may be expended in noting his blindness is only as much emotion as we apportion to animals. It is not on the same scale as the emotion that should be evoked by the similar plight of a human being. Therefore we are prepared to respond later, when we pity Shannon and pity Caesar, too, in spite of revulsion at what he has become—with a realization, *these are only animals*.

And this realization triggers a second—that the same pattern of corruption and violence is infinitely more terrible when it is imposed on humans. So, when we realize in the conclusion of the story that Mrs. Placer has, to some extent, managed to corrupt the girls as she corrupted Caesar, we understand the monstrosity of what she has done. We see it, though the author has not had to tell us in so many words how it happened, or even that it happened.

Seeing this, we understand how the opening is tied in with the whole mechanism of the story. It has provided

212

a unifying scale by which all the events and persons of the story may be measured. This is the sort of addition an author may make to the unities that he discovers to be inherent in his subject.

Plot, character, tone, and theme may all be adapted as the composition progresses, with the object of enhancing the unity of a story. A unified point of view, a unified set of symbols, and a disciplined consistency of language may be imposed by the author as it becomes increasingly clear to him what qualities must be stressed and which excluded from the subject that was in his first conception so indefinite in outline.

Plot unifies by disciplining the action. In forming a plot we ask not only what kinds of action might the characters have performed, but which of those actions would have direct bearing on the outcome of the story.

Character unifies by requiring a concentration on the significance an act or condition has to a particular person at a particular time in his life.

We have already noted that "In the Zoo" is unified by its thematic comment on the relation between persecutors and victims. We must understand that this kind of unity represents both a discovery by the author and the imposition of a preconceived abstract idea on the plastic substance being molded into a story. A unified "point of view" in a story means that the complications, characters, and acts are seen as if through the eyes of one person. In stories told in the first person everything is related as if it were seen by the character who calls himself "I." The use of a first person in telling the story has the advantage of imposing a strong, somewhat artificial unity on events, time-spans, and fragmented actions that have very little natural unity or coherence.

Stories told in the third person may be unified by the point of view if the author reports only what one of his characters would have observed or thought about the events in which he participates. Chekhov sticks to what Gurov saw and thought in "The Lady with the Pet Dog." We are told what he does in the intervals between his meetings with Anna. We are not told what she does nor her state of mind during these absences. If Chekhov had made use of her point of view, the unity of the story would have been loosened.

There is no rule that says a story must be told from a single point of view. In novels it is quite common that the point of view of more than one character is used, and there are a good many excellent short stories where the same is true. It seems to be the case, though, that the absence of the unity which a single point of view provides must be compensated for by strengthening other unifying devices.

A unified set of symbols is such a device. "Symbolism" is a broad topic, and perhaps in our time unnecessarily confused by many critical debates. Without at this point entering any of the complexities of those debates, we can say that a symbol is some concrete element of fiction that "stands for" something else that the author chose not to represent directly. Or perhaps it stands for something that can be recognized intuitively but which cannot be represented at all by straightforward exposition.

For instance, we will note that in "The Lady with the Pet Dog" the appearances of nature (weather moods particularly) stand for the changing climates of Gurov's interior life. We are permitted an intuitive glimpse into the sub-rational states of his psyche by the author's device of showing us the surrounding weather. The moods of weather and landscape change. They change from the melting languors of Yalta to the "good-natured" frosts of Moscow, the dank fog of Anna's provincial home, and the heavy fall of snow in the concluding section.

Chekhov's consistent reliance (delicately inserted, never

insistent) on the weather to hint at Gurov's psychic state provides a unifying element in the story. The symbols here are so worked into the general texture of action that we readily understand that the changes in weather are not mere observations of the story's physical setting.

A more ambiguous symbolism runs through "Sandra." In this story I believe we are to read "slavery" as a symbol of the whole man-woman relationship of our times. (For his satiric purposes the author needed a term that could be spread to include *love, marriage, courtship, dependence,* and the other terms that are normally used to give a realistic account of this relationship.) Without here going into a detailed analysis or interpretation of the story, it can be asserted that a consistent observation of the ironic relationship between "slavery" and the usual terms was an absolute necessity for disciplining the fantasies of which the whole picture is composed.

Language is never a "pure" element in literature. Sometimes we speak of it as if it were a coat of paint put on the surface of the story, coloring the bulky objects of character and setting and livening up the action. Of course language is all there is in a story. Language is the material that is arranged and fitted into the author's design.

And yet, just because of the all-encompassing nature of language, we have to speak of it sometimes as if it were only another one among many ingredients assembled into a finished story. In speaking of the language of a particular piece of fiction and in considering it as a unifying factor, we mean that certain limitations on vocabulary and usage have been accepted. The limitations do not prescribe what words will be used—that depends on the material and the way the author uses it. They merely rule out certain parts of the author's full vocabulary as being unsuited for the story in hand.

Stories told in the first person must evidently be confined to a vocabulary representing the natural usages of the character who tells the story. When the character is hardly articulate or when his experience is limited, obviously the vocabulary of the story will have to correspond to his limitations. But even when the character is represented as highly articulate—the narrator of "In the Zoo," for example—language should be kept so consistent as to give the illusion of a single *voice* maintained from beginning to end.

If we experimented we would find that a good many of the expressions and sentences in "That Lovely Green Boat" could be inserted into the body of "In the Zoo" without altering the voice or producing any discord. But there are others that do not seem at all to be spoken by the same person, and it is in noting the things that could not be transposed that we can become most sharply aware of the distinct personality of language in each.

It should never be assumed that the voice in any first person story is the author's own natural voice. This may be the case, but the chances are that the author has at least assumed a role for the occasion and has maintained the language of that role for the sake of a unified effect.

In third person narration a similar limitation of vocabulary may be adhered to for the sake of unity. An old maxim has it that "the word should be a cousin to the deed." This means, obviously, that if the circumstance being told about is simple, the usable word is the simple word. If it is earthy, an earthy word is best. If it is surprising . . . a breathless word. And so on.

This is a very good principle, but something must be added to it when we attempt to write good fiction. The word must be cousin not only to the deed but to all the other words that recount the sum of deeds in the whole piece. In even the shortest of stories the princess may go from the elegance of the palace to the humble, dusty field and back again. Actions pass from delicacy to violence and back again. And if language is always adapted to the thing it is momentarily expressing, the effect may be chaotic.

One of the hardest things for an inexperienced writer to accept is that his very best passages of writing may violate the unity of language that his story needs. But there is only one answer to this common conflict: when some local bit of excellence jars with its context, it has to be thrown out for the sake of unity.

Remember always that the writer's task in transposing reality into fiction is one of discovering a unity, a focus, in the endless, unceasing flux of experience. After that he imposes as many unifying devices as he can in the process of composition.

You will find that as you write, and as you consciously try to heighten the general effect of unity, one unifying device will conflict with another. An attempt to unify the symbolism will strain at the unity of the point of view. Unity of time or of setting will make it difficult to give a proper emphasis to the thematic unity, as one expressive value bids against another for the reader's attention.

With these inherent conflicts every writer does the best he can. One thing is subordinated for the sake of another. Something suffers so something else will not be entirely obscured. Constant compromise, constant adjustment is the very essence of the creative process.

And its aim—beyond the effect to be obtained from any particular device—is the feeling of unity in the whole story.

For it is this over-all unity, beyond anything else, that works a kind of magic on the reader. It persuades him, for a while, not to look at the world as an incessant stream of data, but to enter the concentration that emotion and form can give to mere events. It is the unity of a story that enforces the reader's empathy. Fiction has no sensational means for shocking the reader into an abandonment of his own identity. But when it is most beautifully unified it can tease him, for a while, into willingness to stand on an island in the flux of time and suppose that the experience told to him is his own.

6

Plot as Unity

A plot is one among several of the unities in fiction. Readers never see it in a pure state, for in a story it is trimmed, compromised, and adjusted to other elements for the sake of the unity of the whole.

However, in some stories, plot is flaunted on the surface while other ingredients are disposed of in brisk, offhand fashion. If such stories are usually low grade, we cannot make a rule that declares them all to be, for emphasis on plot should depend on the conception, on what the author has to say.

Sometimes the plot is so subordinated to other things that its function as an expressive or unifying device is evidently of small importance. It is then merely a hanger, on which more valuable goods are displayed. In some other cases—and this is often true of first-rate contemporary work—the plot is so elaborately interwoven with the other threads of fiction that its presence is only detectable under a determined scrutiny.

I can imagine, for instance, that a sensitive and responsive reader of "In the Zoo" might receive much of the impact of the story and much of its meaning without becoming quite aware that it *had* a plot. Such a reader might

219

say, "It's just an account of two women recalling a painful stretch of their childhood. It's another of those *New Yorker* stories that depend for their effect on being so very well written and so candid in rendering miniature grief."

For such readers we may assume that the plot has done its work without being detected. And perhaps there is no higher tribute to the author's skill than to say she has so successfully hidden her principal expressive means.

The plot is obscured in this story because it does not open when the story opens. The first scene of the story is part of the end of the plot action. It is only in the flash-back, beginning with a mention of the town of Adams, that our attention is subtly diverted back to the point in time where the plot may be said to begin.

It does violence to a beautifully integrated story to seize the inwoven thread of plot and pull it out to examine it in isolation. But that may be the briefest way to demonstrate that it is really there.

Roughly, the plot of "In the Zoo" is this: Two orphaned sisters come to a small town to live with a woman who runs a boardinghouse. The woman, Mrs. Placer, makes them miserable by her tyrannical and self-righteous supervision. *So,* they seek a partial escape by making friends with Mr. Murphy, a small-town caricature of Saint Francis, the patron saint of animals. *Because* he recognizes what they must suffer at Mrs. Placer's hands, he gives them a dog to ease their loneliness. *Because* any natural affection for man or beast seems to Mrs. Placer a criticism of her witchy puritanism, she destroys the relationship between the girls and their dog by corrupting the poor beast into her own image. *So* when Mr. Murphy learns that his charity has been frustrated by the witch, he goes with the children in the quixotic hope of setting things right once more.

Because Murphy has dared rebel against her sly (but powerful) tyranny, Mrs. Placer sets the corrupted dog to kill the monkey Shannon.

This wanton slaying *motivates* the half-demented, good old man to poison the dog. *Because* the sly Mrs. Placer has tricked him into a realm of action where he is insecure and where his justifications are undemonstrable, Murphy is the chief victim of the rebellion against her. He has killed one of the animals he is bound to love because he could discover no other means of striking at the invulnerable Mrs. Placer.

Because the girls have been committed to witness his terrifying defeat, they in their turn make a final submission to the insuperable nastiness of their guardian. ("Flight was the only thing we could think of, but where could we go?") If Mr. Murphy was in the wrong—and obviously Mrs. Placer had put him in the wrong by forcing him into killing the dog—then the girls, whose most generous sentiments allied them with him, were in the wrong, too. (". . . Gran . . . held us trapped by our sense of guilt.")

So, because they are trapped by guilt, the girls are transformed into accomplices of the woman and the spirit of denial that has made them suffer so much. However much they may resent being accomplices and grieve that they have come to this, they must recognize what they are.

The action of the plot ends with this recognition.

There is the plot of Miss Stafford's story in its bare essence. It seems to me a powerful and terrible plot—in Aristotle's phrase, it inspires "pity and terror" even in the unadorned form I have given it.

Is it not a grim parable of all rebellion, a sort of pessimistic revision of the story of Don Quixote—since here the quixotic Mr. Murphy hardly accomplishes more than to deliver his followers to the evil enchantress? In Cervantes' novel there is more than a suggestion that, after all, the knight of the rueful countenance redeems his world by the indomitable spirit of his folly.

Whoever has seen the shape of modern war will find this plot a poignant reminder that in crusading to kill the tyrants of our century, soldiers of the good cause have been most notably successful in massacring the tyrant's victims.

Yes, this "hardly noticeable" plot turns out to be strong enough in all reality once we take the pains to isolate it.

But how and why did the author obscure it as she has? First of all, how?

1. By separating the opening of the story and the beginning of the plot action.

2. By allowing the plot action—which is firm and continuous in itself—to fade out of focus now and then. The reader is given a close, clear view of part of it. Other parts, and perhaps the most telling parts, come to the reader obliquely or only by the inferences to which he is compelled. In fact the most important phase of the plot, the transformation of the children into accomplices in Mrs. Placer's evil, is not as directly told as the part about Mr. Murphy and the monkey.

3. By shifting the pace of the narration so there is little connection between it and the pace of the plot action. By allowing the story to branch off into tangential scenes and half-scenes that do not belong in the causal sequence of plot action. The episode in which Mr. Murphy throws a stone at the boy teasing his parrot is wonderfully effective—but quite outside the plot. So are some of the bits about Mrs. Placer among her boarders.

4. By establishing a tone in the opening and concluding scene (the "envelope" around the long flashback) that is at ironic variance with the grim fatalism of the plot.

Now, why were these displacements of focus and emphasis on the plot made? (In finding justifications for the special adjustments made here, we can get some insight into the process of composition. We can never know, of course, how many of the author's choices were rationalized, how many were intuitive. We can make an informed guess as to which could have been dictated by reasoned controls imposed on the material.)

1. The opening of the story provides some engrossing hints about the over-all significance of the action to which we will presently turn. Since the scene of the opening is continuous in time with the scene at the end, it actually represents the resolution of the plot action, though the reader is not in a position to see that clearly until he has finished the story. In a way that provides suspense, the scene is fashioned to hint where the action is tending until such time as the action declares its own goal. See, here is the punctured target, the author says. Now I will take you up the range and re-enact the firing of the shot that struck it.

2. The action of the plot is really a very extensive one. To have kept it all in sharp focus—by developing scenes and groups of scenes—would have meant to build it into a much longer work. It might have been a novel. It would have had to be a novel if the author had not so magnificently solved the problem of compression by showing us, in one episode, the pattern that was essentially repeated in all those imaginable episodes treated sketchily or left to our imagination. Once the encounter between Murphy and Mrs. Placer has taken place, we are made to understand the fatal pattern. Then the task of the rest of the story is merely to establish that this pattern was inevitably repeated on a larger scale. In saying that the transformation of the children into accomplices is the most important phase of the plot, we are not saying that it represents the kind of material that could be given concrete representation. The transformation is subtle—the sort of thing which, in reality as in fiction, we grasp better through inference than through observation of concrete acts. Therefore, the author wisely left that process to be inferred once the pattern it must follow was made clear.

3. Given the decision to leave much of the plot to be

gathered in by the reader's inferences, it would seem necessary to surround that part of it which is demonstrated concretely with a profusion of fragments suggesting the complexity of appearances beneath which the essential pattern was repeated monotonously. All the departures from the main plot line serve as a kind of compensation for the author's tactic of leaving so much of the plot unstated. She relies on the reader's imagination to fill in the empty stretches. At the same time, the reader has to be stimulated to imagine a turbulence and variety to prevent his conceiving that the plot worked as a subhuman mechanism would. Life does present a kaleidoscope of appearances to our eye, even when our eye has been conditioned to read a simple significance into all those that fall within a given range. The shift of pace is another tactic of compensation for having compressed so extensive an action into a short story.

4. In a somewhat different direction the flip, mocking, less-than-tragic tone of beginning and end help to place the "bleak tragedy" of the flashback in a context that we can accept as representative of whole lifetimes. The grimness has indeed spread through a pair of lives like a stain. We are supposed to believe that everything the sisters have experienced has been to a degree contaminated by the stamp Mrs. Placer put on their character. And yet—could we believe that there were not occasions of better and worse, of laughter as well as despair, in the lives that are the subject of the story? *To a degree* the curse was always present. By indicating that the degree has been variable, the author has actually strengthened the force of her statement, since she has taken these pains to disarm our skepticism. We might indeed be shocked and impressed by a bare, straightforward presentation of the plot. But if it were bare, wouldn't we keep some reservations and tend to protest, "Oh, it couldn't have all been *that* bad"? By foreseeing such reservations, perhaps the author has gained

some advantage over them. Has been able to say, "Still, worse than you would like to think. . . ."

Indeed, all the adjustments and subordinations of the plot in this wonderful story seem to me to strengthen it. "What's lightly hid is deepest understood," says a poem of Richard Wilbur's. Here the light camouflage and the significant gaps in the plot help bring it alive and burning into the reader's heart.

Another bit of praise for this deft management would be to point out that it contributes to the lifelikeness of the story. Lifelikeness has no direct connection with plot. But it is a virtue in itself, and a story from which a plot obtrudes awkwardly is not likely to commend itself as a true picture of life as we experience it.

One more thing—at a certain point of understanding what the author has done here, we can feel a purely aesthetic appreciation of her skill. Quite apart from the content of fiction, its movements, subordinations, the establishment and dissolving of formations, and its harmonious progress can give us the kind of satisfaction we get in watching a well-rehearsed group of dancers on a stage. This mechanical control exercised by an author might be called the "choreography" of fiction.

Is it better to talk about a thing for a while before recognizing the need to define it? Or better to define it first and then try to respect the definition in subsequent discussion? I am not sure. I know that in the ordinary course of things we do both, and that in the ordinary course of things we edge—not always directly, but sometimes like a boat tacking into the wind—toward broader and more useful understandings.

I realize I have been talking about plot in this chapter and elsewhere without yet defining it. And the truth is that I was a bit wary of attempting a definition too soon for fear that the way I defined it might rouse some defensive prejudices that would hinder communication.

Since each of us began to read fiction we have known what plot is. Alas, we seem to know it is different things.

Somehow among readers and critics—and among teachers of fiction writing, too—there have grown up "pro-plot" and "anti-plot" factions. The pro-plot people are bent on condemning fiction which, according to their measure, lacks plot. (It is distressing to find that by *plot* they often mean no more than a particular plot, often closely associated with a standard kind of subject. For instance, in a western story, unless the plot involves a conflict between a gunslinging stranger and a corrupt, wealthy landowner, there might appear to be no plot at all.)

The anti-plot people contend that plot is a mechanism that destroys the life in sound fictional material. They are right only in that this *sometimes* happens. Of course it need not. When plot is properly integrated with the over-all unity, it can be first among those elements that give the illusion of life to fiction. For people are actors. Their nature is action.

And plot—plot is no more and no less than a causal sequence of action.

Note that it is not a mere sequence. We have no plot when we say, "Bertha tinted her hair red. That night she dined alone." We have a plot—or rather the small beginnings of one—when we say, "Being too timid to let her friends see that she had dyed her hair, Bertha dined alone that night." The causal connection between dyeing the hair and dining alone is established in the second example as it is not in the first.

Yet we must note, and be very clear about it, that the causal connection between parts of the whole plot action is very often not stated explicitly. When we outline a plot in isolation from a story, the connections will probably be obvious. When we integrate a plot with other elements, the connections will often be shown indirectly, principally by the altering situation, intent, or emotion of the characters.

In paraphrasing the plot of "In the Zoo," I italicized the words expressing causal connections. However, in the story itself one looks in vain for such drab mechanical linkages. The plot has been, so to speak, dissolved in the fictional medium. But it has not lost its coherence. The links between the parts of the action are all the more impressive for being revealed in the behavior and emotion of the characters instead of being stated by the author.

By supplying and italicizing the word *because* in my paraphrase I meant to demonstrate not only the links of causality, but the continuity from beginning to end of that causal chain.

This continuity is essential to the unity of a plot, but something more is required, a rounding out of the sequence. It is easiest to comprehend plot unity if we look at examples and think of the unity as being rounded out when the questions raised at the beginning of the action are all sufficiently answered by the action that follows. In "Sandra" the rather insignificant plot comes to its natural end when the narrator has made a trial of each of the principal choices that follow the purchase of a female slave. In "The Best of Everything" there is a resolution of the plot action when Ralph demonstrates the place on his scale of values that will be occupied by the woman he is going to marry. The action of "That Lovely Green Boat" is rounded out when the young people destroy the fragile loveliness that rested momentarily in their keeping.

After we sense the natural "rounding out"—the unity—of some passage of causally related action, we see that its part in the general unity of the story comes from its relation to the needs, desires, and purposeful or capricious choices of characters. The original step in the action of a plot very frequently comes as the response of a character to the situation he must confront. The stimulus provoking the response is what we call motivation.

The significance and complexity of motivation may cover a vast range of intensity. If my leg itches, I am moved to scratch it. If Othello becomes suspicious of his wife, he is moved to resolve his suspicions and know the truth. But however important or unimportant the motive, we can hardly think of the action of a plot without acknowledging that it proceeds *through* the passionate decision of characters.

This is true whether the author chooses to use much space in examining the motives of his characters or leaves them to be inferred by the reader. We must never judge the profundity of fiction merely by the author's profundity in examining motives. Their best usage is in serving as the link between character and action. The question of how much motivation the author must supply seems to me best answered by the answer to another question: How much is needed to make the action proceed meaningfully out of the characters?

Criticism—and this means your judgment as you are writing a story as well as your estimate of someone else's work—must draw some fine measurements in determining sufficient motivation for a plot action. We know from personal experience that some things seem to "just happen." These include not only the things that happen to us, but those actions for which we must assume full responsibility before the law and before God. Not all of life, by any means, is shaped by those actions we undertake because we have a reason to. Yet, at the other extreme, the picture of an action that unrolls without being checked or furthered by the full choice of one or more characters seems altogether inhuman and therefore not the proper concern of fiction.

There are absolutely no prescriptions for the proper degree of motivation in any particular story. At the misty border where character melts into action and action stimulates changes in character, the author has a particular responsibility for declaring his own view of life. In Thomas Hardy's novels, motives do not count for much against the sweep of an impersonal fate that drives his characters against their will. (In *Jude the Obscure* the chief character quotes Aeschylus: "Things are as they are and will proceed to their destined end." What people may wish or attempt will have little consequence, Hardy seems to say in most of his novels.) "The Yellow Raft" quite obviously minimizes the weight of human motive, reducing it to an importance no greater than that of the forces that coincide to lift each of the innumerable waves and swells of the Pacific.

I am afraid it is not so easy to find, in the literature of this century, examples of the opposite extreme. The effectiveness of the personal will is not a theme to which most contemporary writers incline. But it is possible to find, in the novels of Jane Austen, perhaps, or Dickens, or George Eliot, a considerably closer tie between personal motive and the consequence of action.

Plot is a device of expression as well as a means of unifying the subject material of a story. It expresses the author's belief about the nature of human destiny, the importance of will in determining the shape of events.

An author may "make the action come out" this way or that way. Strictly within the possibilities of the material, Miss Stafford might have structured her plot so it would have made an entirely different total statement. Suppose that, instead of causing Murphy to poison the corrupted dog Caesar, the author had told us Murphy stole him back from Mrs. Placer and disappeared into the mountains with him. Evidently this sequence would have suggested to the engrossed girls a way out—a general vision of rebellion and escape—that they could hardly have construed as morbidly as they did the poisoning. Therefore they would have been diverted to a future less bitterly restricted than the one we are made to witness.

(Incidentally, I am sure this would have made a poorer story than the one we have. I hasten to apologize for such gross reconstruction of so fine a work of art. But I trust that I have shown how the meaning would at least be *different* if the plot were altered.)

To take a more famous example and distort it even more grossly, let's imagine that the plot of *Madame Bovary* is changed. Instead of winding herself more and more tightly in the moral and practical snares of adultery, Emma Bovary finds the means to thrive and nourish both wit and charm by taking a succession of lovers.

Then what is in its present form a tragedy would become a comedy. If Emma Bovary brought herself to a ripe, autumnal serenity instead of to hysteria and suicide, the spirit of the book would be closer to eighteenth-century optimism and rationalism than to the glooms of nineteenth-century pessimism.

But would it also be closer to the truth about adultery and its consequences? There seems no fixed answer to such a question. One writer in one time might have said yes, another in a different time, no. And the only moral we can make from such speculation is that the shape and outcome of the plot are the prerogative of the author. He will manage them to express what he believes to be the truth he has found on his pilgrimage.

Which does not mean that he may be capricious in his arrangement of the plot. Ordinarily plot must follow lines of probability. But usually in every plot there are a very few strategic points where things might be made to go otherwise than they do. A little luck this way, a little luck that way and the whole course of a life might be altered for better or worse. This principle is as true in fiction as in the life it imitates. As true, but no more true.

Complete caprice in shifting the course of plot action merely destroys the fundamental virtue we expect of a plot, its consistent chain of causality. In making such central shifts in the plot as I have suggested are possible in *Madame Bovary* or "In the Zoo" the author would have found himself under the obligation to "earn" the different outcome of the action by a series of alterations in character, tone, language, and in the sequence of the plot following the point where the crucial change was made. The better the integration of the plot with the other story elements, the more true it is that one change makes others obligatory.

Remember this in revising your own work. Up until the moment you are ready to declare your story finished, the plot ought to be considered tentative or provisional. It's yours to reshape until it expresses your conclusions about the way life goes. But as it is fused with the characters and situations of your invention, they make their own claims on it, too. Those claims must be satisfied in revision.

Often plots are praised for their "inevitability." This means the reader is convinced that if event *A* took place it is nearly unthinkable that it should not have been followed by *B*. Once *B* has happened, then *C* must follow. Now of course any writer is in a position to be skeptical of the inevitability of any plot. He knows that after he has written *A* into his story, he could follow it with *E* or *J*—with *K* or *X*. At a certain point of composition when his materials were still fluid in his mind, the arrangement of events could be determined by pure whim.

Yes—at a certain point. The same is true of love. "Love has no conscience," says one of Shakespeare's sonnets. It may, as well as not, begin with a whimsical choice. "But who does not know that conscience comes from love?" The reasons for a whimsical choice in love or in forming a fictional plot begin to develop *after* a choice is made. And you will find that they assert themselves with ever more rigor as the various elements begin to fall into place.

We may agree with E. M. Forster that plot is fiction "in its logical, intellectual aspect." Plot expresses the author's judgment on the way life goes.

Very well. But we are writers, not retired sages. If we have any fixed logical and intellectual judgments about

231

life—life in general—we will find them only remotely valuable in evaluating the particular phase of life about which we have chosen to write. Prejudgments and preconceived plots are apt to be arid or pompous, simply unfair to the material on which they are imposed.

Judgment—and therefore the shape of the plot itself—ought to come from an engagement with experience, in this case the experience of writing. Plots are found as meanings unfold to the writer. A good writer is a sort of midwife to his plots, not a dictator. He helps them emerge—take shape—from character and situation in the way his logic and intellect tell him action *would* emerge in life as he has known it. Judgment should be completed only when the story is fully formed.

It seems to me the best of practices to begin writing a story before you are quite sure what the plot will be.

Of course it is possible to work out a very definite plot before making a real beginning in the language of the story. Perhaps for some writers at some times this may be the most effective approach. The trouble with such a method is that once you begin to add flesh to a predetermined skeleton of a plot, you are almost certain to find that other elements have to be cut and distorted arbitrarily to fit a design which might become nonsensical if it were altered. No matter how experienced the writer, I think he cannot foresee all the nuances of character—their force or weakness, which have so much to do with how they would act—until he begins to develop them within the environment of the story. So to commit them in advance to actions for which they may be imperfectly suited is like the folly of trying to staff a complex enterprise by taking names at random from a telephone book.

All the elements in a story must be, as it were, "consulted" before the writer dares make certain decisions required to give the finished shape to his plot. He makes some initial declarations, arising from his conception. He writes down that his characters have done something. But

232

then he pauses to consider who these characters are and what they might *want* to do next.

Yet, in urging pauses for consultation, I don't mean that characters can be allowed to dictate their own fates. There are writers who say, "I begin by creating characters. When they come to life, they write the story for me." I doubt if this is ever quite the whole truth. If it were, such a method could probably not result in a unified piece of fiction.

Characters make their own demands. So do other elements. But against all these pressures (never ignoring them) the mind of the author goes on urging the demands for continuity and unity of the plot. One requirement is pitted against another, and the story grows the way a vase rises on a potter's wheel, with one hand inside and one outside, both helping to determine the form.

It is not the pressure for a plot, but that pressure plus whatever in the material resists it with its own demands which results in the best plots.

It follows from this that the best plots turn out to be somewhat of a surprise to the author. They have come, of course, from those conceptions that are the roots of all creative work. But as they grew they put out branches and leaves that could hardly have been guessed at until the actual work of composition was done. They represent an achievement of logic and intellect not won in a vacuum but won in a struggle with the recalcitrance of unformed experience.

The happiest mixtures of motive, chance, and unconscious determination probably appear in plots whose outlines were clarified in the process of writing. Why? I don't know exactly, but I'll offer a theory: It may be that the act of writing a story is, for the author, a subtle kind of parallel to the action of his plot. That is, his plot is a disguised account of what happened to him as he wrote. The objective action he describes is a counterpart of the subjective struggle required to shape ideas and get them down on paper. Ernest Hemingway writing about an old man in a boat holding onto a line attached to a great fish he can't see may be writing about Ernest Hemingway composing *The Old Man and the Sea*. So it may be that all the good plots of heroes in action are, in some sense, self-portraits. Not only that, they may be self-portraits of the author committing himself to this very work.

Is this a fanciful theory? I don't mind your thinking so if it has suggested to you the kind of involvement required to make a living plot. In the last chapter I suggested that a concept begins to unify when the writer sees himself as a kind of supernumerary character, responsible to the fictional situation in the same way as the other characters he will put into it.

I believe that the creation of a plot is merely an extension of this initial sense of personal involvement and responsibility.

When a writer's intuition tells him that what *is* happening to himself as he imaginatively shares the peril of his characters *would* be the next thing to befall them, he is in a position to reveal the deepest truth he knows by shaping the plot according to this intuition.

7

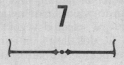

Character

As I write these chapters I am often amused at how easy it would be to sound as if I were writing a cookbook: "Lay out all the ingredients on your worktable. Take a large, well-greased unity of conception. Line it with a short crust of plot. Next prepare a filling of character. Don't skimp. If you have some left over it may be served up in patties for tomorrow's meal."

It's ludicrous of course to assume that recipes for fiction can be given like recipes for shepherd's pie. But I'm not afraid of sounding like the author of a cookbook, when and if that might help explain part of the process of writing.

After all, a book about writing is not the same thing as fiction itself. Fiction ought to appear before a reader like a stage performance—all neatly organized, rehearsed (or revised) to a fine economy, graceful and flawless in the illusion it offers. But in talking about fiction we go intentionally backstage. We see the makeup being applied. We see the stagehands hauling props around, and maybe the actors are helping them. Back here there is not supposed to be illusion, but only a job to be done. So who cares if he sounds more like a cook than an artist, as long as he helps with the job?

In creating character in fiction, first you take a character from observation to which imagination has been added (make the filling out of selected vegetables, brown gravy, spices). Then you fit this large and lively concept of a person into the confines of the story (fill the lower crust just to the brim and add spices; then put on the top crust).

In any case—however unlike cookery the fictional development of character may be—it seems that we must distinguish two steps in the process of carrying an image of personality over from life into fiction. We're obliged to recognize these two steps because of the difference between life and the art of language.

In real life, character is revealed to us; in fiction, character is created. *There* is the difference between experience and artifice.

One begins by drawing from life. The writer knows or has known some actual person whose qualities suit the role left open for someone in his general concept of a story.

We know that a great number of the best fictional characters have been drawn from life. Biographers delight in telling us which members of the family, which friends, and which enemies served as models for great authors. In *Anna Karenina* Kitty is drawn from Tolstoy's wife. Emily Bronte drew her brother Branwell in creating the character of Heathcliff in *Wuthering Heights*. Surely Flaubert used his mistress Louise Colet as a model for the portrait called Madame Bovary. In the gallery of autobiographical characters, Levin is Tolstoy's self-portrait. Stephen Dedalus is Joyce's.

All this is true, as far as it goes—and it doesn't go far enough to satisfy the writer confronted with the problem of how to get Uncle Harry—or himself—onto the white sheets of paper lying beside his typewriter. You can't just press the old boy onto the paper, like a rose pressed be-

ween the pages of a book. And a typewriter isn't a camera.
You can't get a portrait just by pressing one of the little
nickeled levers.

We've got to ask what it means when we use the figurative expression "drawing from life." It means first of all
observing a person, noting his history and his appearance,
his bank roll and his mustache. It means achieving, to the
extent we can, some sense of identification with that person so we know, intuitively, what it means to him when
he says "I." (I realize how great and complex an effort
of the imagination is required to achieve such a sense of
identification, even though I'm mentioning it briefly here.
Fortunately, though, this capacity for identification is something we don't have to learn in class. It's part of the gift,
great or small, that the individual writer hopes to discipline
by reading books like this or otherwise rationalizing his
inherent capacities.) Though scholarship has determined
who is the principal model Flaubert used in writing of the
adulterous wife of a country doctor, we would know
much too little about the process of creation if we could
not grasp what Flaubert meant by saying, *"Madame Bovary, c'est moi."* ("I am Madame Bovary.") He meant that
he had passed from observation of externals to a knowledge of "I" as a desperate woman.

After observation and (when possible) a kind of identification, one still has to do more than feed the results of
experience into a story like sand fed into a bag. We must
not suppose that Louise Colet was the only model for
Emma Bovary. Several other women contributed, including the unfortunate wife of a country doctor who had been,
in reality, a student of Flaubert's father. From one woman
the author drew mouth, eyes, insecurity, and the tendency
to daydream, we suppose. From another he got those memorable fingernails and an unruly temper. From still another came the body and the outrageously trusting naiveté.

A fictional character—and particularly one who occupies a central position in a sizable work—is a composite, then, like so many of the other elements in fiction.

What determines which are suitable among all the characteristics available to a writer with a good memory and several models for a single character? Well, the plot, for one thing, gives some useful indications of what is required in a particular role and what is inappropriate. That is, if the plot requires a woman to cuckold her husband with a vain ladies' man, it must be obvious that the woman can't be given characteristics of tranquillity, obedience, or good sense. She has to emerge as the composite of those characteristics that would make such an action seem probable, and only those.

It is not necessary to think of plot as a dictatorial preconception imposed by the author to see that it always acts as a shaping and selecting influence in the development of characters. In some stories it is evident that characters have been mutilated to fit plot requirements. Obviously this is bad art. But even when it takes form at the same pace as the characters grow, plot restrains, limits, and gives definition to those characters.

The qualities of a character are also selected and shaded by the rest of the cast. The adulterous wife must be made to fit with the particular husband assigned her by the story, and with the particular seducer. In developing the whole cast of characters for his story, the author is a bit like a hostess planning a party, inviting guests who complement each other. The author has, though, the privilege and obligation of literally shaping the people he wants— not merely exercising a hostess's tact and judgment.

But, given an original conception of character and certain limiting requirements within the structure of the story, still more is required to make the artifice of fiction *seem* a true reflection of life. (You see, we are getting farther and farther from the rather silly notion that writing could be prescribed like cookery.) There ought to be, in a story, some quality of decision that will give the illusion that the characters are acting on their own volition. In "The Lady with the Pet Dog" Gurov is "already" bored with Anna after their first adultery. Yet the very naiveté and remorse that seem so boring in the woman are the qualities that will presently make him fall in love with her "really, truly—for the first time in his life." It amuses him that she considers him, at first, to be "kind, exceptional, high-minded" when he has treated her with the "coarse arrogance of a happy male . . . twice her age." Yet he will seek his own humility in an attempt to become what she erroneously thought him to be.

We can explain these expressive, ironic turns in the story by saying that the author's observation of life had shown him similar ironies. And we know that Chekhov "made things turn out" as he did to express the discrepancy between a man's superficial intentions and his underlying will. There is, beyond doubt, the imposition of a preconceived design on the material of this story. And yet it conveys to us the illusion of life because we feel that in the course of writing it Chekhov underwent the change of emotions that he attributes to Gurov—that the nice, bearded, passionate author at his desk must have said, "But after all *I* love Anna for the very qualities that amused me in the beginning."

One senses that almost magical (and yet common) submersion of the author's identity in the identity of his chief character. Logic and intellect and practice as a writer are all superseded while the author believes, *"I am Gurov. What I have been doing in permitting him the action that has taken place thus far in my story is permitting myself that action. Next I will do this . . ."*

Of course no author ever completely gives up his own identity in the creative process. Chekhov knows he is Chekhov even when he chooses as Gurov. And when he has finished playing Gurov's role, he will look back over his work with the cold eye of the craftsman—striking out one passage and adding a calculated effect to polish his story. But unless he has known the moment of identification, when author and character are one, his labors of revision will be partly wasted.

It is probably these moments of identification that weld character and plot together in a perfect fusion, even if each has come from a separate process of thought, even if the plot was loosely determined a week before the character was settled on. Without such fusions, fiction is something less than art.

So, wouldn't it be wonderful if identification of author and character guaranteed perfect fiction? But it might mean only that the writer had perfected a way of daydreaming on paper. When the author is Chekhov—a conscious master of his craft who knows very well how to mesh the elements of his story before he yields up conscious control —great fiction results. In the case of a writer who has not yet learned how to mingle character and action in a design of language, identification is often no better than self-indulgence.

Let's go back from the pinnacle of the art to some fundamentals.

It is fundamental for the writer to remember that:

1. A character in a story is an artificial construction.

2. A character is composed by certain combinations of the basic elements of fiction—language, descriptions, actions, dialogue, and interaction with scene and other characters.

3. A fictional character is not alive in the same sense a human being is, but in a parallel sense. The character "lives" in the environment that the author builds for him, not in the limitless world of actuality.

Let's illustrate these points by reference to the stories included in this book.

First: The frightful and vivid Mrs. Placer ("In the Zoo") is frightful and vivid and funny to the reader *be-*

cause the author, guided by her own notions of the frightful and funny, made her so. The reader does not really
ask, *"Was* there such a person?" He believes that there *is*
such a person because the author has forced him, temporarily, to accept the artificial world of the story as the only
reality that concerns him. Helen ("That Lovely Green
Boat") is not a real girl. We will never see her. We will
only see words printed on a page. But we will remember
her *as if* we had seen her (or even more vividly) because
Mr. Berge built up an artificial association of girl with
river, summer, green living things, and *green boat.* No one
but the author made this association. He made it by hitting certain keys on his typewriter, by striking out certain
words on a manuscript and replacing them by others,
by selecting from among all the possible associations of
sense imagery in the natural world those specific ones that
would evoke this memorable image of "young girl." If he
were making lilies out of crepe paper, wire, and wax he
would not be producing objects more artificial than his
story.

I stress the artificiality of fiction and the comparison
with the flower maker because it is important to remember that writing fiction *ends* in a construction resembling
nature, just as flower-making does. No one praises badly
made artificial flowers just because their maker understood the horticulture of real plants. Similarly a story cannot be praised or valued merely because the writer *started*
from sound observation or profound intuition of human
nature. Observation and intuition have to be artificially
structured within the limits imposed by the medium of
fiction before they will communicate to a reader a sense
of what was once observed or intuited.

Second: Observation of human character is structured into fiction by various kinds of descriptions. "[Helen] stepped
down into the boat and settled . . . like a great blue heron

241

feeling for land under her when she's coming in to land big and awkward against a rough skipping wind." ("That Lovely Green Boat")

Mrs. Placer is "possessive, unloving, scornful, complacent." "We could hear her protestant, litigious voice defending our right to be orphans, paupers, wholly dependent on her. . . ." And "the townsfolk allowed that Mr. Murphy was a drunk and was fighting Irish, but he had a heart and this was something that could never be said of Mrs. Placer." ("In the Zoo") These descriptions, of course, do not tell the whole truth about these two characters—they only supplement other means of character revelation. We ought to note that the particular language employed in them (two sorts in these samples—the author's prose and the speech of the townspeople) also shapes the impression the reader receives.

" 'Isn't he funny?' " Grace's roommate says of her fiancé. " 'He says "terlet." I didn't know people really said "terlet." ' " ("The Best of Everything") This scant and off-hand description of Ralph by a girl who has had little chance to observe him may, indeed, do little by itself to characterize the husband-to-be for us. But, as it is structured into the story, it prepares us for the monstrous shock of revelation at the end. Then Ralph, in the full flowering of his callousness, will ask his bride, " 'Mind if I use ya terlet?' "—and the shocked reader will see that this man regards his woman as no more than a vessel into which he can relieve himself. Then, I suppose, we are in a position to grasp and evaluate his character.

An author's knowledge of his character is built into a story by the actions the author requires him to perform. When Mr. Murphy nearly kills a pestering boy with a stone, we measure the fury of love the old drunkard has concentrated on his animal pets. This is an action that is completely unnecessary for the plot, yet it makes its contribution. The plot action—for example Murphy's poisoning of the dog—establishes the man's character even more forcefully.

When the narrator in "Sandra" frees his slave, the rather minimal plot of the story is advanced, but chiefly the action signifies a perplexity and fumbling goodwill in the character. Here, of course, we are dealing with character in a fantasy. Perhaps the main thing we should note is that there must be consistency in the development of fantasy characters as well as realistic ones. The choice to liberate Sandra must bear the same relation to probable human behavior as the other acts of which we are told. It represents a distortion of reality. It must be distorted no more and no less than anything else.

Gurov's trip to Anna's home town ("The Lady with the Pet Dog") establishes the irrationality underlying his agile intelligence and prefigures the victory of love over the sterile self-image he has trusted so long. The trip is essential to the advancement of the plot—but we know the plot could have been forced to the same conclusion by the use of some other episode. Of course the other possible plot linkages would have done less to round out an image of a particular sort of man discovering his fate than the one the author chose.

Helen's panicky destruction of the green duck boat ("That Lovely Green Boat") shows the peculiar response to guilt of a young girl dazed by her first sex experiences. The revelation here is not a straightforward one. The author has not gone into the minds of his characters to weave a pattern of guilty thoughts, nor has he told the reader plainly that anything "happened" between Richard and Helen when they went in among the maples along the river. The omission of certain information that might have been given permits us to assume that they might have had intercourse or might, at the opposite extreme of innocence, have shared merely the intimacy of being hidden together. But, whatever we assume, the subsequent destruction of the duck boat indicates it was enough to alienate Helen from her childish and delicate relationship with the narrator. I don't mean she destroys the boat on purpose. Rather this act seems part of her attempt to deny that anything has changed. If she can save Richard's boat then all will be as it was before, won't it? She seems to be asking something like that. And if it is impossible for us to put a hard and fast rational interpretation on what she does, the vagueness and confusion of her motives help render a girl of a certain age and temperament—a wild and innocent person discovering that womanhood will be a trap as well as a blessing.

In fiction as in life, dialogue communicates the feel of a character. In peculiarities of speech we detect subtle qualities of personality that expository language could hardly express. When the dog Caesar kills the monkey ("In the Zoo"), we hear Mrs. Placer saying, " 'Why Caesar, you scamp! You've hurt Mr. Murphy's monkey! Aren't you ashamed?' " This speech puts a peak on the scene in which the woman's murderous hypocrisy displays itself. From her own lips we hear the tone of invulnerable serenity in which she accomplishes evil.

The flat and simple dialogue of the young people in "That Lovely Green Boat" does not hide but rather reveals the delicate, fierce turmoil of adolescence.

> "It was a good race," I said.
> "Uh-huh."
> "But he doesn't know his boats."
> "He's got a motorboat," she said.
> "But I beat him rowing."
> "I've got eyes," she said.
> "Did you want him to win?"
> "It was a race. I wanted to win."
> "Well you won."

"I suppose you let me win," she said, mocking me with the tone of her voice. She looked at me for a minute with her mouth open. "Darn you. Darn you if you did."

In this passage jealousy, stubbornness, reticence, pride, affection, and uncertainty are revealed without being particularly designated by the author—and of course all these things are traits of character supplementing the revelations of other parts of the story. It might be worth spending an hour of analysis on this one superficially simple exchange of dialogue to determine exactly which lines express the characteristics I have listed. Of course it is better studied in the context of the whole story than in isolation.

Consider this fragment from "The Best of Everything":

"Nice," he said, feeling the flimsy material between thumb and index finger, like a merchant. "Very nice. Wudga pay fa this, honey?"

How many things can we isolate that work here to characterize Ralph the Beast Bridegroom?

We note the accent indicated by phonetic spelling. (Remember, this is a very risky device. Use it with great caution in your own work. Be sure that it is as appropriate as in Yates's story.)

We note the placing of the question about price—which indicates that Ralph is a man who equates all values with money values. A thing is worth its price to him and nothing more.

We note also the extremely narrow limits of his vocabulary—and note with repugnance (given the circumstances) that the vocabulary has no relation to a sense perception. Not only does he feel the goods like a merchant; he seems incapable of registering the color or texture of the garment in any association with the color and texture of the living body it contains. We are led to anticipate the insensitivity with which he will use that body.

245

It should not be necessary, in "reading as a writer" to linger over every fragment of dialogue to analyze it as I have analyzed these. Nevertheless the reader who does not pause, now and then, to enumerate the revelations of character in good dialogue will miss half the pleasure of reading—and learn nothing useful to himself as a writer.

In mentioning the associations built up between Helen and green, young, summery things ("That Lovely Green Boat") I have already touched on the way in which the interaction of personage and setting can heighten the sense of character. The same thing can be found in any successful story.

The cunningly humorous parallels between animal and human qualities drawn by Miss Stafford represent only a part of the examples to be found in her story. The children's life in the boardinghouse full of grotesques prepares us to grasp the "mesh of lies and evasions" in which "Daisy and I . . . lived . . . baffled and mean, like rats in a maze."

These rather abstract words characterizing the girls in their adolescence would not be so fully packed with meaning if the author had not taken time and pains to show us the maze of boardinghouse intrigue in which they lived their childhood.

The business milieu and the picture of "nights out with the boys" in "The Best of Everything" help the reader grasp the characters of Grace and Ralph. If Grace were not partly shaped in the image of her occupation, already broken by it to the habit of submission, how could she endure the prospect of giving herself to Ralph? Her gratitude to her boss for small gifts and favors comes from the same personality defect as her final determination to go through with the marriage. And Ralph—well, the horror of it is, we feel, that Ralph is little more than the product of sessions in a bar watching the fights on TV.

Third fundamental point: To illustrate that a fictional character is an artificial mental construct that can only live in the fictional environment created for him, we can draw most effectively on examples of fantasy. Sandra, I suppose, will seem to the reader to live. He will believe in her submissiveness, her sulkiness, her affection, her pneumonia, and her pregnancy—as long as he believes in a world that contains a "Federal Slave Board" and male consumers who shop for slaves as routinely as they shop for automobiles. That long and no longer. So in order to make his fantasy of Sandra the slave effectively operate on our imagination, Mr. Elliott was obliged to construct every part of his fantastic world into a temporarily believable—at least consistent—continuity.

"I had four choices, as I saw it: divorce her, have her psychoanalyzed, kill her, or return her to slavery," says the narrator. Now, the first three of these choices are available to a husband in the world as we know it. But it is the inclusion by the author of this fourth choice in the series that is required to sustain our belief in Sandra as a living character. Without that fourth (fantastic, unrealistic) choice to make up part of the whole environment, Sandra would lose her distinct shape. Figuratively speaking, she would die like a fish out of water.

In *Gulliver's Travels* all the little men and the giants would die (for our imagination) if the *relationships* between them and Gulliver were not scrupulously observed in every detail of the story.

Eudora Welty's highly stylized stories about the South show the same principle vividly. Here the question is not so much one of fantasy as of exaggeration in the tradition of the tall tale. Yet her method is an evidently artificial one. There could not be in any actual community of the American South such a uniformly grotesque set of people bearing such uniformly colorful names as her tales declare. And yet, one is not much prompted to question the truth of her stories. Within each of them, the same degree of

247

distortion applies to all details, personages, and actions. They live harmoniously with and draw credibility from each other. Break the tissue with inconsistent passages or details of a purely realistic sort and the whole artifice would become meaningless.

Now, with such illustrations in mind, let me say flatly that the principle is just as true in respect to the realistic story as it is to fantasy or other obviously artificial modes.

Consider what seems to be the "flat"—that is, un-adorned, undistorted, and certainly unromanticized—real-ism of "The Best of Everything." We will probably say, after reading it, that we know people like Grace and Ralph, Mr. Atwood and Eddie. We have heard people talk as they talk. Therefore we may make the easy error of neglect-ing the author's labor in selecting, arranging, and ordering his material, the author's pains to keep the progress of revelation and action consistent—in other words, we may overlook the artificiality of the story and thereby ignore the art.

Suppose we rearranged the exchanges of dialogue ar-bitrarily. To give a very small example, suppose that in the last scene Ralph asked to use the "terlet" as soon as he came into the apartment. (As indeed he might have in real life, being full of beer.) The particular suggestiveness of his request which, as it stands, gives such a terrible sense of human callousness, would be totally lost. Sup-pose we put the conversation with Eddie after the final scene with Grace. (Ralph's insensitivity makes it easily conceivable that he might have been as moved by Eddie's generosity after leaving Gracie as he was before he saw her.) We would have no sense of how easily human beings can be distracted from the possibilities for happiness that lie within their grasp.

The arbitrarily rearranged material would still be as "true to life" in its scrambled form. The dialogue would still "sound" real. But once the author's artificial (artful) arrangement of his material is gone, so is ninety percent of the profound revelation of reality. We would have mere surface details, fragments of sociological data from which the pathos and vibrancy of life were gone.

Perhaps the artificiality of fiction is a secret we writers should keep to ourselves. Don't tell readers. Let them believe they are looking at life as it really happens when they read our realistic stories. But we must never fool ourselves.

Almost every story contains a number of characters. Some of them are little more than names. Others have things to say, bits of action to perform. Some—frequently one or two in each story—are the excuse for the story's existence. We see events through their eyes, or see them as if we were riding on their shoulders. What they do, see, and feel is the meaning of the story.

To accept the illusion of the story, the reader needs to know these central characters pretty well. Insofar as the design of the story permits, they should be made into "round" characters. That is, we need to show not merely their primary passions and motivations, but some of the hesitations and equivocations that are not altogether lined up with their principal drives. This character wants to make a fortune. Good. That's his main drive. But he won't cut throats to do it. That complicates things. He is relentless in his ambition. But susceptible to the diversions of love. That too complicates things—and is, very briefly, what is meant by showing a character in the round.

Rounding a character obviously makes him more lifelike, therefore more interesting. So it would seem at first thought that the thing to do is round out and complicate every character in a story. To the extent that this is done, the story would be improved, wouldn't it?

No. It would spoil the design of the story, destroy the over-all unity. Round characters are part of the design of

249

a good story, but so are flat ones, characters in whom there is no complexity.

In "The Best of Everything" it adds to the story that Gracie is dubious of the marriage *and* determined to go through with it. That Ralph is sexually attracted to her *and* unable to recognize her invitation. Without such degrees of roundness the story would mean little. At the same time, to keep proportion, to allow Gracie and Ralph their place in the center of the scene, it is necessary that Mr. Atwood be left flat as a stereotype and that Eddie should appear as the single-minded oaf, without the depth or variety within his character that such a person might have in real life.

Obviously the problem of flat and round characters is different in novels than it is in short stories. The novel simply offers more space for the author to show the variety within his characters and, if he wants to, to develop more of them in the round than he could in a short story. But basically the principle is the same. Flat characters are required as foils for the ones more fully rounded.

Needless to say, flat characters should not be dull characters. In "The Lady with the Pet Dog" Gurov's wife is a stereotype of the Russian intellectual female of her day. Anna's husband is a "flunkey." The two of them hardly appear on the scene of the story. Yet they are rendered with such sharp observation that they are a significant part of the whole unity. They are exactly what they have to be to help us see Anna and Gurov and their motives for adultery.

Sometimes it seems that the minor, flat characters in short stories amount to no more than a single epithet— "the fat man," or "Mr. Beaver, the timid boarder" or "Helen—the watchful eye." Seeing that they are only puppets made of a few words—and that still they may give a sense of lifelikeness within the whole unity of the story—the writer is reminded of the most important fact about his craft.

All fiction characters are made up of words. Observation begins the process. Identification—acting out the part —carries it along. But finally it is choice of language, the artifice of design and relationship to other fictional elements, that makes the character live for the reader.

8

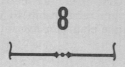

Tone

The writer is the man in the middle.

Like a man trundling a wheelbarrow between a sand pile and a waiting truck, the writer works between his subject matter and his audience. He shovels up a load of experience and vision. He delivers a story.

He has responsibilities to both subject matter and audience. He must be true to the fundamental truths his observation provides. He must be true to the capacities of his audience. He has seen something. He must now make a structure of words that will re-create his original vision for people whose interests are not quite the same as his. He must "put on a show" to communicate what was originally not a show at all, but was perhaps a hidden, rich vein of ordinary life.

He must rely, then, on some tactics that might be called theatrical. He must produce effects. He must engineer surprises. He must exploit to the fullest the communicative possibilities of tone.

Tone is the principal theatrical element of fiction. Plot and character drawing, artificial as they may be, are inherently the means by which a writer discharges his responsibility to his subject matter. A plot, however little it resembles any action the writer has witnessed, must still *represent the kind* of action that takes place in the world of his experience. He can only measure the truth of his created character by reference back to actual people he has known. But tone is his direct assault on the expectations of his readers. Or we might call it his conversation with readers.

We know from ordinary conversational experience that the same episode, involving the same people, may be told in different ways, each of them producing a different effect on the hearer. The tone of the speaker's voice may be sarcastic or sympathetic, awed or contemptuous.

The use of tone in conversation is analagous to but not entirely the same as its use in creating fiction. In a sense, by exploiting tone we have got an actor to read our lines and heighten them by inflections. However, the use of tone in fiction is more limited—but finally much more subtle and resourceful—than the effects that can be contributed by a living voice.

The use of lighting effects in the theater is also analogous to the manipulation of fictional tone. The background music in movies is a similar device from another art. We know how emotional receptivity can be heightened by such music. The Indians are about to appear over the edge of the butte. Tense, rapid, loud, brassy music rouses all our memories of danger, fear of the unknown. The Indians charge down the slope clothed and armed with all the terrible weaponry that the audience can imagine for them.

Fiction lacks the powerful mechanical supplements of tone that the movies and the stage can draw on to set the imagination of the audience at work to help communicate the story. But fiction has the quiet, inexhaustible resources of language itself. Whatever the shape of plot or characters, an author has the duty as well as the opportunity of choosing language which will condition the reader's receptivity to them.

253

It seems useful to distinguish a number of ways in which language may be used to produce tonal effects.

First it produces them by an appeal to sentiments. Certain words will generally evoke sympathy for any object to which they are applied. Other words or combinations of words will evoke suspicion, distaste, or dismay. Obviously, when Ralph is called a worm—"a white worm" ("The Best of Everything"), or Anna's husband is called a "flunkey" ("The Lady with the Pet Dog"), the author expects the reader to respond with antipathy for these men. (Single labels like this are not, of course, final judgments on any fictional character. In fact, one of the tricks available to a writer is to rouse a preliminary antipathy for a character and then win the reader over to approval. Such play with the reader's responses is what I mean by *theatrical* maneuvering.)

The significance of labeling Ralph's friends as "the fellas" is not quite so obviously a cue for the reader to pass judgment. To call a group of friends "the fellas" is ordinarily innocuous enough. But in the context of the story (and the effect of words always depends on their fictional context) the innocuous sentimentality shows up as evidence of sexual and intellectual immaturity with sheer cruelty as its consequence. In using the cliché term "the fellas" the author has added a tonal effect to complement the meaning of the action.

It would take months to point out the wide, complex range of tonalities in a story like "In the Zoo." (The value of spending so much time, though, might be indicated by saying that this wonderful story would be a drab, sparse thing indeed without the tonal modulations of a superb stylist. The difference between first-rate fiction and drab failure is worth investigating for months, is it not?) One short passage will barely suffice to illustrate the constant theatrical play of the author's style. Yet an analysis of such a passage will take all the space I can afford to give it.

This passage will be found near the end of the story. It refers to the warps of personality the sisters are still suffering some time after Murphy's monkey was killed. They are working at a dude camp.

"I can still remember . . . overhearing an edgy millionaire say to his wife, naming my name, 'That girl gives me the cold shivers. One would think she had just seen a murder.' Well, I had. For years, whenever I woke in the night in fear or pain or loneliness, I would increase my suffering by the memory of Shannon [the monkey], and my tears were as bitter as poor Mr. Murphy's."

I trust it will be self-evident that the author is appealing to our sentiments in behalf of (1) the narrator, who guiltlessly suffers fear, pain, and loneliness and shares the grief of bereavement with someone she loved, (2) the monkey, and (3) Mr. Murphy.

The reader with normal human sympathies will not hold them back in reading this passage—though he probably ought to if earlier events in the story had not shown that these words refer to substantial suffering. If they did not obviously refer to such previously documented suffering, they ought to be dismissed as sentimentality, since by definition sentimentality is emotion in excess of its cause. Here the cause of suffering is enough to justify an appeal to the sympathy of the reader.

But yet, not all the expressive, theatrical devices of the language in this passage are accounted for by pointing out those words that make us sympathize with the victims of cruel self-righteousness.

The author, in her superb cunning, has seized on the reader's willing sympathies and forced them to a higher pitch by an interesting manipulation of hyperbole.

Hyperbole is exaggeration. And if we pause to think coldly about the passage and the event it principally refers to, we will see that it *is* an exaggeration to call the monkey's death "murder." Common sense balks at that term. When a dog kills a monkey in a small town, it may be news. But *murder. . . ?*

No. The act was not a murder. Common sense is right.

But, under the spell of Miss Stafford's style, common sense has been superseded. The exaggeration, we feel, is truer than a flat common sense statement—"the dog killed the monkey"—would be. For what the exaggeration means is that in her knowledge of Mrs. Placer's role in that death, the narrator saw a literally murderous process at work. Objectively speaking, nothing died except a monkey. But the play of language reminds us that objective fact is not the real subject of the story. The significance—not the fact—of Shannon's death is what the story gives us. The theatrical effect of exaggeration in the quoted passage helped to force the real subject into the reader's mind.

Exaggeration of the kind just pointed out is one of the perils—but also one of the richest potentialities—of the language we lump under the general heading of rhetoric. Rhetoric is "high-flown" language. It contains emotional overtones and suggestions not necessarily present in the objects or events it refers to. It "says more" than is required to convey the sensuous appearance of objective acts or things. The danger in its usage is that it may say so much that is superfluous to communication that the reader will take it for mere wind, mere indulgence of a large, sloppy vocabulary.

The opposite of rhetoric—but just as much a distortion of common-sense reporting—is understatement. As the term implies, it means the author has chosen a language so sparse, so clipped, so uninflected that the reader is almost obliged to say of the events and characters described, "By gad, there must be more to this situation than meets the eye." And his imagination is provoked into supplying interpretations that the author's language steadfastly refuses.

The stylist who employs understatement works like a boxer who feints in order to draw a punch from his opponent. Then, if he is a real stylist, like Hemingway, after he has provoked the reader into action, he counterpunches. Just as much as the rhetorical writer, the understater means to control the imagination of his reader. Both of them are using tonal, theatrical effects.

And somewhere in the middle, between rhetoric and understatement, there is the undistorted style, the realm of language that neither exaggerates nor minimizes the values of the events that fiction presents.

Ah, you will say at last, the undistorted style must be the proper style for fiction.

But is it?

Not necessarily at all. It might be usefully pointed out that the pre-eminent writers of American fiction in the last third of a century have been Hemingway and Faulkner. Faulkner's style is clearly a rhetorical one. Of course Hemingway stands almost as the inventor of understatement. There has been much fine fiction in the "middle style," but nothing to quite compare with the work of these two.

Sticking to the confines of this book, I would point out that "In the Zoo" is highly rhetorical. (To my taste it is the best of the stories I have collected.) "That Lovely Green Boat" is essentially an example of understatement. (It does not seem to me least among the stories we are studying.)

Of course it would be a sad day for fiction if the undistorted, "middle" style should lose its popularity. We would then not have enough fine stories like "The Best of Everything" or Chekhov's magnificent study of adultery, or of fantasies like "Sandra" for that matter. The principle that "the word should be the cousin to the deed"—which means calling a spade a spade, and neither "an implement of cultivation" (rhetoric) or a "thing" (understatement) —is the safest principle for fiction. Stylists who shun both rhetorical heightening and understatement seem to serve the principle most faithfully.

But they pay a price for their lukewarmness, perhaps. They do without many—not all—of the tonal effects that are the subject of this chapter.

Of course rhetoric, middle style, and understatement can all serve the purposes of fiction. All can be abused.

When rhetoric is abused, the result is what we call "purple" or "false poetic" language—merely colorful language that hides the subject instead of revealing it by significant theatrical lighting.

Consider this passage: "In daily anticipation of the arrival of her knight on his white charger, Bettina inhaled the languor of her holiday in the scintillating mountains, indifferent to the stiff-jointed antics transpiring among the older guests on the verandah of the hostelry."

Such language might be called nastily poetical. It is not poetic. Any resemblances it bears to poetry are impertinent and totally superficial.

It is purple, overwritten, and corny.

It could not conceivably be incorporated in a good work of fiction, except as parody.

I made it up rather hastily, but I have found something quite like it in dozens or hundreds of over-written manuscripts I have read in my time.

Now consider another passage: "We stood aghast in the dark-red sunset, killed by our horror and our grief for Shannon and our unforgivable disgrace. We stood upright in a dead faint and an eon passed before Mr. Murphy picked up Shannon's body and wove away, sobbing. . . ." ("In the Zoo")

Surely the resonance and drama of this rhetoric will be evident even out of context. In context the language appears to be, at least, harmonious with the language tone

f the whole story. At best, it seems to be *exact* in its
endition of a spiritual, emotional crisis quite beyond the
ower of uninflected language to express.

As supplementary reading, you ought to read Katherine
Anne Porter's "Flowering Judas" and at least the end of
er novelette "Pale Horse, Pale Rider." These are splen-
id examples of a rhetorical style serving the purposes of
modern fiction. So are the final pages of Faulkner's *The
Wild Palms.*

The abuses of understatement are, perhaps, as prevalent
and as easy to fall into as the abuses of rhetoric. If
housands and thousands of manuscripts have been flawed
y purple passages and over-writing, there are just as
many that sound like poor imitations of Hemingway's
classic manner. The imitations differ from the real thing
n carrying understatement to the point that it simply does
ot tell the story the author had in mind.

To caricature the abuse of understatement, let us sup-
ose that *Macbeth* is to be transposed into modern fiction,
nderstated. In Shakespeare's version, MacDuff speaks the
ollowing lines when he hears that his wife and children
ave been murdered on Macbeth's orders:

> " . . . . All my pretty ones?
> Did you say all? O hell-kite! All?
> What, all my pretty chickens and their dam
> At one fell swoop?"

Now this magnificent rhetoric is obviously not a speech
hat we can attribute to a contemporary who hears of the
murder of his family. But if one made him say, instead,
I feel bad about it," the understatement would be abso-
utely ridiculous.

A sense of propriety, a sense of tact must be developed
o curb the abuses of one sort or another of theatrical,
onal exaggerations of language. To a large extent this

tact will grow, at its own sweet pace, as you get more experience in reading. Caution might well be the watch
word until tact has matured. To be on the safe side, th
young writer probably ought to incline toward a middl
style—choosing the language suggested by observatio
of his subject, and the language required to communicat
the real substance of characters and their acts.

Only remember—that the time will come when safet
is the wrong choice. No one takes the pains of learning a
art merely to end up playing safe, any more than a goo
soldier absorbs his training merely to stay safe throug
a war. There are times when only daring will pay off—i
literary expression as well as war. No one can tell yo
exactly when the time has come to risk launching int
rhetoric. That's one of the responsibilities you must tak
on yourself if you want to be a writer really worth readin

I have spent a large part of this chapter talking abou
language as an instrument by which the tone of the stor
is controlled. But evidently it is not language alone tha
determines tone.

An author may make adaptations of plot solely t
modulate tone. The shaping of a single character or th
selection of a cast of characters may have an importar
effect on tone. The novels of Thomas Hardy (*Jude th
Obscure, The Mayor of Casterbridge,* etc.) make goo
illustrations of both these propositions. The unmistakabl
note of grief—the lamentation of a helpless, compas
sionate observer of the human scene—that makes th
novels so memorable would be weaker if the author ha
not forced into the plot some improbable excesses c
disaster to heighten the reader's emotional response. W
know the author is exaggerating when he forces *all* thos
disasters on Jude and Sue. But we catch the tone of con
passion exactly because we note the exaggeration. As fc
the use of character to achieve the tone the author want
note that the presence of good-humored, stalwart mind

characters is a favorite Hardy device for modulating the grimness smothering the lives of his main characters.

Think how the tone (not to mention other elements) of Shakespeare's *Othello* would be altered if he had cast some of his other characters in the situation of that play. If Portia instead of Desdemona had married Othello. . . . Well, of course she might have argued him out of killing her for supposed adultery, but if she hadn't—if Othello had again been so maddened by Iago's lies that he must kill—the tone of the whole play would be different. It is precisely Desdemona's sweet submissiveness set in a contrast of opposition to Othello's rage of love that leaves a special tone ringing in our minds when we forget some of the actions of the plot.

Turning to the stories in this book, can't we see that Richard Yates has used his plot ("The Best of Everything") to twist the screws on his female character? Hasn't she been slapped a bit more brutally than mere realism would require? I think so. And I think the author forced this tone of brutality to express a pity for women that would otherwise be inexpressible.

Can't we see that William Berge has used the character of Carl (who is neither particularly interesting in himself nor useful to the plot) to maintain a note or tone of boyish stoicism that keeps everything *pianissimo,* keeps everything quiet enough so we can hear the thin, sweet lament for the passing of first love? I think so. And I must say I also think the use of Carl for this purpose in the story is one of the most masterly examples I have to show you of character selection as a means for tonal control. (Go ponder Berge's story again.)

To sum up the observations of this chapter and make them, if I can, useful to you as a writer, let me say that you must not think of tone as a paint job applied to an otherwise finished automobile. Tone is not "added to"

261

a story after character, plot, and so on have been completely drawn.

No, it is part of the whole process of selection that goes on while you are composing a story. Shall I choose this character or that to add to the cast? Shall I make my characters take this course of action or that? Shall I heighten or understate the language of this descriptive passage, that bit of dialogue? In making every one of these choices, considerations of tone are involved.

In revision, as in the writing of a first draft, you must be aware that tone is a means of emphasizing this part, subordinating that, in your communication with the reader. Sometimes, in adjusting tone, it helps to imagine that you are telling the story to an actual, present listener. Would he laugh if you got too solemn in telling him a particular part of the story? Then watch your language. Don't let it be too solemn. Would he yawn and tap his foot if you told him some episode as you imagine it would really have happened? Then find some language for telling it that will make him laugh or cry, sweat or tremble.

Remember above all that tone is your way of working directly on the sympathies of the reader. It is the delivery of the mail you've toted such a long way. It is a part of story-telling that must not be flubbed.

9

Theme

Theme is the meaning of a story.

It is not the "moral." It is not the revelation made by the final action. It is not to be confused with subject matter.

It is what the author has to say about his subject matter. It is expressed by all the material and the formal devices incorporated into the story—which add up to the over-all unity—but it is not exactly the same as this unity. It is related to the unity of a story as light is related to a light bulb. That is, theme *comes from* the unity of a story as light comes from a carefully made mechanical implement.

We would need to know little more than this about theme if we were reading for pleasure or reading as critics. (Though experience and attention would be required in order to grasp the theme of a well-done contemporary story.)

Since we are reading as writers, we want to understand as much as we can of how the pursuit of meaning—of theme—enters into the process of composition. What is its part in the imaginative effort that begins when an author chooses a subject?

In all probability, a vague, powerful glimpse of the meaning inherent in a subject was what led to the choice of that subject in the first place. (In Chapter 2 we began to examine the act of writing by comments on the choice of subject matter. Now we have spiraled back to considering what may precede that choice. Do you feel that we are progressing backward? Good. A writer's progress must be backward—toward the sources of his knowledge and imagination—as well as forward to a disciplined control of his craft.)

Purely for the sake of illustrating how theme may be both the beginning and end of the story-telling process, let me describe the way "The Yellow Raft" *might have been* conceived—how its theme might first have risen in the author's mind.

He is—let us suppose—either remembering or watching with his own eyes planes flying far away over the Pacific Ocean. Suddenly the notion comes to him: *How strange it would be if the Ocean were watching this scene as I am watching it.* How strange those planes would look if, for a minute, I could forget they were occupied by humans like myself, with whom I am identified by certain bonds of sympathy and concern.

(Surely notions like this occur to us all from time to time as common experiences repeat themselves, suddenly seeming less familiar than we would have believed. It is when common things seem all at once full of wonder that a theme is born in our minds.)

From the vague notion that all human endeavors—like the "conquest of the sky" on which this century prides itself—would look wonderfully different if seen by non-human eyes, certain other fanciful conjectures follow naturally. One's non-writing friends might well call these conjectures *idle*. Never mind. They are part of a writer's work. A writer has the questionable privilege of working while engaged in activities that would be sheer loafing for anyone else.

It may have occurred to Connell that the whole history of air warfare in the Pacific would look strange—and therefore wonderful, horrifying—if it were viewed by eyes and an intelligence disconnected from the sentiments of patriotism and human compassion that ordinarily colored our understanding of combat over the emptiness of the real ocean. How strange, wonderful, and horrifying to watch the planes that disputed the Solomon Islands, the Marianas, Truk, New Britain, Ulithi, and New Guinea without knowing that the pilots were "avenging Pearl Harbor" or that, in their Quonset huts at night, they wrote love letters to their girls, played poker, and told dirty jokes. How odd the vanity and pity of war would seem to eyes that knew neither vanity nor pity.

From speculations like this—Wordsworth called them "intimations" and whatever we choose to call them we will recognize that they are essentially thematic, essentially the perception of meanings—the author's mind may have begun to narrow its search for a subject.

After the recognition that vanity and pity are merely human additions to the mechanism of the universe, the author's imagination may have begun to churn up the materials appropriate to the recognition of this particular theme. He might have remembered the vanity of men relying on their splendid, intricate fighter planes equipped with all the modern devices for use in emergency. *Then* he could choose a circumstance in which all the precautions to forestall emergency failed.

A fighter plane goes down in the water. Its armor and weapons and all the skill that went into its manufacture cannot save the wounded pilot from being dunked. A yellow raft is released from the sinking plane and the pilot manages to get aboard the raft, endure a while, and set off certain distress signals. They fail to bring help. When help comes—in the form of the cruising patrol plane—the pilot has disappeared from the raft.

That is the subject matter of the story. It appears to me

to proceed directly enough from the original set of fancies which I have pretended were the author's. At any rate, given the meaning which unmistakably guided the writing of this story, such a subject, such a particular incident, is the apparently inevitable choice.

The subject matter is given a certain minimal structure of plot. The plot is a very uncomplicated one, but its ruthless inevitability helps express the theme, emphasizing the vanity of reliance on safety devices.

There is no character in the story. That is, there is no human character. To withhold character from fiction is to make an unusual formal alteration, since normally we expect character and plot to be interwoven. This very noticeable peculiarity seems to have been dictated by a preconceived theme, and permits the author to suggest, delicately and economically, that the Ocean itself, or some equally pitiless observer, is watching this frustration of human vanity. And the absence of a pitying observer becomes in turn a tonal device—a form of understatement that forces the reader to contribute pity.

The tonal devices of language seem equally to have been dictated by the thematic intent of the author. He has seen —perhaps from the moment his imagination was stirred to begin a story—the ironic discrepancy between a sentimental view of the air war and one from which all passionate concern had been removed.

Note the exploitation of that irony in this passage: ". . . a blister slid open near the tail of the Catalina, and a moment later a cluster of empty beer cans fell like little bombs in a smooth glittering trajectory toward the sea, splashed, and began filling with water." The comparison between the beer cans and bombs suggests that to the observer divorced from humanity—to the witnessing Ocean, perhaps—there is no significant difference among the objects falling into the water. Bombs or beer cans, sandwich papers or fighter planes, men riding their rafts n an agony of hope or yellow rafts disintegrating into ragments of cork and rubber—all this debris is the ame to the Ocean.

Now it must be plain that the carefully considered anguage of the passage I quoted cannot have been fully ormed in the author's mind at the moment he had his rst intimation of what the story must mean. Of course he whole process of writing—formation of plot, charcters, language, and all—is required to mature or ripen theme. Nevertheless, the thematic intent must be present, a however unripened a form, to guide the mind of the vriter through every stage of composition.

It is perhaps the most fundamental of the principles of election indicating which one of several choices an author aust make from the possibilities open to him.

I think it is no less than the beginning and the end of tory-telling. It is what dawns in an author's mind before e chooses his subject and sets his expressive devices to vork.

It is what is left, like a resonance, in the reader's mind fter he has recovered from the emotions he felt while eading and even after he has forgotten the shape of the lot and the illusion of life contributed by characters— nd after language has done its job and is folded back in- the printed book.

When a writer succeeds in re-creating for a reader his rst wondering perception of a theme, then communicaon of fiction cannot be matched by any other art. When e reader is brought to a consciousness of wonder like e wonder that once invaded the author's mind, and says f the shared intuition, "I agree with you," the job of ction is done.

If you have read the other stories in this book as atentively as you should have, you will already have rasped the theme of each. And putting that theme in

words other than the words of the story itself is not alway
satisfying. It makes the theme sound like the "moral" o
the story sometimes, and that is unfortunate.

Nevertheless, purely for purposes of analysis—to ope
up the imaginative structure of the stories so we can pee
inside—I will set down a tentative statement of theme fo
each.

That Lovely Green Boat says: First love is too fragi
and fugitive to bear the demands of actuality. (Conside
ing all the elements of the story, decide for yourself whic
ones help most vividly in making this statement.)

The Lady with the Pet Dog says: A man can stumbl
into the humility of love through the arrogance of lus
(Is there a similar theme in other stories or novels yo
have read recently? Can you write a story on a simila
theme? Please don't make the error of writing anythin
merely to *illustrate* a theme, however wise or importan
that theme may sound to you. But if a theme from some
thing you have read strikes a responsive spark in you
imagination, tend the spark and see if it will light up int
a story from your own experience.)

The Best of Everything says: Marriage can be a doo
as savage as a blood sacrifice in spite of the sentimenta
ties that accompany it. (Doesn't the relentless movemer
of the story toward the final disappointment suggest th
passage of a condemned woman on her way to the plac
of punishment?)

Sandra says: Neither bondage nor freedom is a solu
tion to the problems of a man and woman living as
couple. (Obviously the most important thing to study i
this case is the way fantasy is used to state a theme th
could be expressed by realism.)

In the Zoo says: The destruction of innocence is th
likely result of blind, self-righteous bigotry. (How does th
title help to make the point? Does it suggest that the worl
is a kind of zoo, in which people are kept like cage

animals? Are Mr. Murphy's animal pets representatives of innocence?)

It is possible, I suppose, to write a story without a theme, though I have suggested that stories often begin to shape in the writer's mind when the theme flickers into his consciousness. It is not only possible but common that the theme of a story may be shallow or commonplace. It is a good idea to review your own work a few days after it appears finished—after you've given your mind time to cool—and ask, "Does it mean anything?" Do you still find in it, approaching as a reader, that insistent spark of meaning from which the story sprang? Does the material really mean what it seemed to mean while you were in the heat of writing? It is by no means unusual for a writer to miss the potential significance of his work while he is busy putting it together. Part of the process of revision consists in probing for that significance by reading and considering one's second thoughts. The next step is to add whatever is required—another character, a more exactly chosen phrase, another step in the plot development, or a bit of narrative preparation—to heighten that significance.

A writer hopes to be neither obscure nor tactlessly insistent on a point that will seem mundane to his readers. I suppose that between these extremes it is better to be tactless than obscure, but both are faults that can be refined away by experience as writer and as critical reader of your own work. Maintain the habit of comparing your own work with accomplished professional work—with the stories in this book, for example. Don't be too savage with yourself in making comparisons, and don't let your work off too easily. And realize that in this matter of theme—the ultimate statement of your story—perhaps nothing but a shrewd comparison will tell you how far you have succeeded.

10

The Novel

Fiction is a free and easy art compared to poetry or the drama. In the matter of distinguishing between short stories, novellas (or novelettes, as they are just as often called), and novels, no criterion except the simple, pragmatic criterion of length has ever been firmly established. And this criterion probably didn't emerge from reason or aesthetics, but from the practice of publishers or the habits of readers, to which writers conformed.

Ordinarily we consider that a short story is any piece of prose fiction with a length of one to fifteen thousand words. Anything shorter is probably a joke, an anecdote, a vignette, or a sketch. Beyond this length fictions are labeled novellas unless they exceed a loose boundary of about forty to forty-five thousand words. If they are longer than that they are novels.

There are formal differences between short stories and novellas or novels. At least there generally are, but it is perhaps not very useful to try specifying these differences because of the huge variety of approach possible to any of the lengths. We say that a story is to a novel as a submarine is to an industrial complex centering in one city but linked with several others. The economy, the adaptation of one part to another that is characteristic of submarine design is also characteristic of the short story. The sprawling profusion of an industrial complex is like the profusion of a great novel.

That image is not very specific. Neither will this chapter be. But I hope that both may provide the beginning of illumination.

Nearly everything that has been said in the previous chapters ought to be as true of the novel as of the short story. The requirements of plot, character, theme, and so on are not different in kind, though they may arise in different forms and admit to some different solutions.

But before beginning to write a novel the young writer ought to think of this: A novel's length makes it a project in which one must make major investments of time and effort. More is lost when the effort bogs down or goes astray. Also, I suppose that some writers who haven't yet mastered the fundamentals of their craft take the expanse of the novel as an excuse for avoiding the solution of problems that must be solved quickly in a short story.

Therefore there are a lot of advantages in learning to write fiction by practicing with the shorter form. For me, there is something incomparably sad about a novel manuscript—the result of a year's work or more—in which language, scene, and character are inadequately handled from first to last.

Writing short stories gives one the chance to try his hand at different ways of telling a tale—first or third person narration, more or less objectivity, more or less dependence on dialogue and dramatized scene, understatement and rhetoric. Without experience in various kinds of story-telling, a writer is forced to depend on luck and his native gift to see him through the composition of a novel. Luck is fine, of course, when it runs your way. In fairness to himself, one might well choose to add experience and discipline before too much was at stake.

After offering such caution, I ought to add at once tha
writing a good novel may be easier than writing a goo
short story—at least it will be so for some people, afte
they have reached a moderate level of technical pro
ficiency. A certain amount of the mental agility and th
skill with language required for the shorter form may b
compensated for by other capacities in writing novels
The novel obviously offers easier opportunities for expanc
ing characters, actions, or ideas up to the point at whic
their meaning will be fully revealed.

Apparently some people will find themselves more a
home in writing novels, others in writing short stories. It'
partly a matter of temperament. And the whole motive i
writing such a book as this is to encourage you to make
number of trials so you will find what you are tempera
mentally suited to write.

Choosing a subject for a novel may be quite a differer
matter from choosing one for a short story. As I said i
the last chapter, sometimes the poignant intimation of
theme may indicate an excellent subject for brief trea
ment. For a novel something else is required—enough de
tailed experience with the subject matter to fill in
more complete scene peopled with a larger, more full
developed, cast of characters.

The subject of "The Yellow Raft" would hardly do fc
a novel. It is almost inconceivable that even a story c
much greater length could work without some depictic
of character—and character is not part of Mr. Connell
subject.

And yet it readily occurs to us that the story, ver
much as it stands, would serve beautifully as part of
novel. These few pages might have been the ultimat
concluding scene of a novel about some young men—
maybe they are called Jack and Norm and Scoop—wh
took part in the early battles of the war in the Pacific. N
one can stop us from imagining such a thing—or goin

on to imagine that the pilot who clings to the raft a while might be Jack. The poor devil came all the way from his New Jersey home and a boisterous sad circle of high school friends to die like this in the middle of the empty ocean.

Probably the ordinary reader does drift on to such imaginings, amplifying what the author has provided, drifting by a kind of inertia after the powerful shove that the story has given his thought and emotion.

For the writer—who is also a reader—this means simply that ideas for novels may very well originate in reading short stories. Very probably, though, the most fruitful ones will come from reading his own stories. This is true for the very good reason that his stories came—or should have come—from his own experience and that they have not exhausted it.

Our imagination might indeed fall under the compulsive spell of Mr. Connell's story so far that we would get a poignant momentary vision of Jack, Norm, and Scoop in their high school days in New Jersey. But do we know enough about the way these boys turned into men as they went to war to flesh out a novel? Probably, for most of us, the answer is no.

But around one's own short stories lies the great reservoir of one's own experience, which is more apt to be made accessible as subject matter by writing stories from it than to be exhausted, used up, by those stories.

We know that many great novels existed first—at least in the author's mind—as short stories. *The Magic Mountain* was conceived of as a short story. So was *Ulysses.* There are many other examples.

And we must not imagine that such novels are merely padded out or filled in—like beef cattle pumped full of water before being sold—to make them suitable for marketing as novels. No. What happens is something like this: The original conception or writing of the short story establishes a kind of beachhead, a place to land. Onto that beachhead the author concentrates the forces of his imagination, which previously had no point of debarkation. As the beachhead expands it is easier and easier for the imagination and experience to discharge all they have been accumulating through the author's life. The novel grows on territory won by the short story.

I like to see a certain integrity in a writer's growth—and by integrity I mean the growth from something done well to the same thing done better. When a writer can and will rework his own subjects, finding them so much broader and ampler each time he treats them that a new work results, I am confident he has something worth saying. I worry more about writers who skip from subject to subject, never returning to find what they may have missed in the first exploitation.

So my advice is not only to begin your practice as a writer by turning out short stories, but also to consider those stories as your very best source of ideas or subject matter for the first novel you project. A story, or more than one, may even serve as part of the novel. It should go without saying that these stories may have to be altered from what you believed to be their final shape to adapt them to the novel that is growing out of them.

Should a novel be "plotted"—or planned in detail—before the writing begins? Perhaps. Perhaps not. The main thing to remember is that the plot has to be worked out sometime. The finished work must represent the completion of a plan. Some very few writers may find they work best if they completely outline and predetermine the shape of the whole novel. This of course can only be done reasonably when the writer has, at least, the "feel" of his characters and a good sure notion of the meaning he wants the action to embody. Otherwise the predetermined plan will usually choke the life out of characters as soon as they begin to emerge and will reduce the action to a mere manipulation of pawns.

274

I suppose that most writers will find it best to form a general, loose plan for the whole book, a plan that permits the emergence of surprises when the author learns more of his characters by writing about them, a plan that remains tentative until the last revision is made. Without such a plan—becoming more definite as the work progresses—sheer confusion and waste of time are apt to result.

For one thing, there is simply more detail to manage, to keep track of, in a novel than in a short story. In fact it very often occurs to me that the principal gift of a novelist is that of being able to keep in his mind all he has put into his own work on all the previous pages. Without some way to keep track of this detail—and make page 300 consistent with page 30 in what it says about his characters—a novelist may flounder completely.

For another thing, the sheer time required to write a novel presents problems that must somehow be dealt with. A short story may very well be written in a day or two or three of hard work. Sometimes even in a few hours. The chances are that the writer's attitude toward his material will remain unchanged during that period. The distractions of daily life will not interrupt his train of thought so much that he forgets how he meant to make use of details planted on page 2 of the story. This concentration of effort pays off, usually, in a concentration and consistency of effect in the short piece.

A novel, however, is apt to require months, a year, or several years to finish. It is very hard for any mortal —whether he is a student, a teacher, a lover, or the support for his family—to maintain either a consistent attitude toward his material or a memory of all he intended to follow as a consequence of the details written down on page 2.

He begins a novel in November. The cool, crisp weather affects—as it should—both his imagination and his attitude. The year is ending, and it seems a time for detachment, for summing up not only the passions of the past summer but of all the summers gone. In this mood he shapes his characters and moves them through the action of the first chapters. He has made a good start and gets past Christmas in the confidence that by June he will have not only a finished manuscript but one that will be better than anything he has done before.

By the first of April he has been delayed by two weeks of illness; he is depressed by the new world crisis in the headlines; he knows he cannot finish the novel by June. The fine lush weather affects him—as it should not—and he is anything but coolly detached. He is anxious and full of anticipation—not only about what will happen next to his characters, but what will happen next to him. He cannot understand his mood of last November—therefore he can hardly bear to read what he wrote in that vanished mood.

Toward the first of September he is at last working on his final chapters. The promise of relief—of getting the novel off his back and being able once more to live like a human being—has given him a second wind of confidence. A mournful exuberance takes possession of his mind and colors everything he writes in these days. It should not, because the sense of his novel requires here the tragic detachment with which he began, so many, many pages ago. By now he absolutely cannot bear to read the pages written in April. He suspects that they were written by some stranger, who meant to parody his characters and confuse the reader by planting dozens of false leads.

In October he writes the last word.

He takes a month off. Attempts to mend the fences in his personal life. Assures all his friends he did not mean to neglect or insult them during the past year. He sees that he has been foolishly extravagant and foolishly self-denying while he spent himself on his work. He shrugs and tells himself that he can now begin to pay his debts and enjoy life again, because the novel is done.

Then . . .

Then he settles down to read the result of the year's sweat and anguish.

He finds—of course—that it is full of impossible inconsistencies. That the language reflects every personal problem he has encountered in the whole year. The tone of the beginning is not only inconsistent with the middle and end, it is badly suited to the part of the story in which it appears. He sees that his intention changed about four times. His hero has turned into a villain. The girl he once thought virtuous was really a slut all the time.

Then. . . .

Then, I hope he does not burn the manuscript nor take up a career in business. If he is a real writer, he goes to work on the faulty manuscript, ruthlessly changing what has to be changed, rebuilding the whole thing until at last the missing consistency is imposed. If the final work is not as unified as a good short story, written in a single burst, it may still have that larger, looser unity that we require of the novel.

This sketch of a writer in labor with a novel might be beside the point if I had not seen it happen too often. Even novelists of experience go through something like this—so often, in fact, that I'm tempted to think the novelist's task is not so much to master technique or material as to master himself.

I have seen very many promising beginnings go astray because the author could not discipline himself enough to keep the middle and end true to his first conception. At the very best, he wasted precious time by changing intentions as he went along. At worst he made a mess impossible to straighten out.

Now, if it is true that writing a novel often begins like a marriage, with a honeymoon period of confidence and promise, what can be done to keep the novel true to its original promise when the honeymoon is over and the drudgery begins? (There is a large element of drudgery in writing and acceptance of this fact is an absolute necessity.)

One way to keep consistent is to accept the authority of what you have already written. That is, subordinate each new page to the pages that precede it. Keep re-reading up to the point you've reached and make sure that new pages do not introduce anything that is inconsistent with the story thus far told. Hemingway said once that his daily practice was to read *from the beginning* the novel he was working on, then add two or three pages and quit until the following day. Such a practice may be too rigorous for everyone's use, but the spirit of it is very important. It is one way to minimize the distractions of daily living in favor of consistency in the work.

Another suggestion I would make is this: If you have begun to write without a detailed plan, stop after writing forty or fifty pages. Read what you have done very carefully and critically, looking for the design that has emerged from your initial efforts. Analyze the characters and their potentialities, note where the action is tending, decide on a climax logically related to the direction the action is taking—and *then* prepare a very definite plan for the rest of the novel. Write it down. (It's not enough, sometimes, to "think things through." The effort of putting your intentions on paper in outline form may help clarify them.)

Decide when new characters are to be introduced. Decide what changes in fortune will take place to mark the major phases of the action. Divide the coming action into chapter topics if you can. Decide what revelations will further illuminate the characters you have begun to develop.

Note your decisions. Put your notes where you will see them every day you write. From now on, stick to those decisions unless there is some overwhelming reason to abandon them.

This is not a foolproof method for maintaining consistency of intention or quality of writing. It would be quite useless for some writers, too confining for others. I think it has a number of advantages over trying to make a strict plan before beginning to write. It can save wasted effort by reminding the author not to follow each new whim.

Chapters. We know that novels are ordinarily divided into chapters and that each chapter tends to be *somewhat* complete in itself. Each chapter has some degree of unity within the larger unity of the whole novel. A writer's ability to give form to individual chapters and still make each contribute to the larger form is the culmination of technique for a novelist.

A chapter should have some resemblance in form to a short story. Yet, if it is closed and complete in itself as a story should be, there would be no way to link it to adjacent chapters or to material that lies remote from it in the book.

Every chapter ought to have a specific job to do. Suppose there is a character whose importance to the whole novel has been hinted in subordinate parts of several chapters but who has not yet been given a chance to appear. It might well be the function of a whole chapter to bring that character to the center of the stage and let him perform an important act. It might be the function of a chapter to provide a flashback, explaining something that went on before the principal action began. A chapter may bring together two or more characters who have previously acted their parts separately. Usually a chapter will present a distinct new phase in the progress of the major characters.

Each chapter ought to prepare an introduction for the chapter·that follows it. Frequently this preparation is made by leaving incomplete some line of interest that we would expect to be completed if the same topic were presented in a short story. That is, if "The Yellow Raft" were actually to be incorporated as a chapter in a novel (as any but the final chapter) it would have to be modified in such a way as to direct the interest of the reader to something outside this immediate scene. At its simplest this could be done by raising the question of the identity of the pilot or the crew of the PBY. Was the man in the raft our friend Jack from New Jersey? Is his old high school rival O'Connor one of the crewmen of the PBY? Is O'Connor remembering the summer they graduated while he drinks his beer and eats his sandwiches and watches for a sign of life in the empty sea?

Answers to such questions would blast the form of the short story apart—but they would open it enough, provide enough loose ends to attach it to preceding or subsequent chapters in a novel.

Division into chapters provides for a change of pace in the development of a novel. If the first chapter is largely scene, the second chapter can be largely narrative. If Chapter 5 opens with dialogue, Chapter 6 should, perhaps, open with a description and go on into narrative. If Chapter 3 ends on a note of suspense, Chapter 4 or 5 might well end on a note of tranquillity. If there are many characters seen briefly in the first chapter, perhaps the following chapters should concentrate on individuals in solitude. This change of pace may seem merely a superficial trick to keep the reader awake. And . . . it may be nothing more than that. But like the other resources of fiction it can be made part of a pleasing and significant design.

Again it must be pointed out that the writer can, if he is diligent, learn more about the way chapters are structured internally and fitted together by reading than by learning abstract principles.

On this point I have a specific recommendation to make: read Chekhov's short novel *The Duel*.

I can think of no more masterful use of chapters in all fiction than you will find there. Each chapter prepares beautifully for what is to follow. Groups and clusters of chapters drive to intermediate conclusions which are in turn incorporated into the movement toward the novel's climax. Anyone who plans to write a novel owes it to himself to study thoroughly the organization of this masterpiece.

As an aid to study of the chapter design, I would recommend diagramming the novel—that is, listing for each chapter the characters whom it depicts, the principal topic or conflict, the unresolved problems left in suspense for later solution, and the characters who are mentioned but who do not appear.

Chekhov was, of course, one of the greatest of playwrights, and *The Duel* is put together with the precision and economy of a piece written for the stage. Not all novels will be or should be put together with such meticulous economy. But every novel presents the writer with organizational problems similar to those that Chekhov solved so brilliantly here.

The story he has to tell is a great one. We assume it might have been told very differently. It would still be a great story, I believe, if far less skill had gone into fitting the scenes together and managing a large group of characters related to each other in complex ways. But even if the story were trivial and the characters shallowly conceived, the organization would remain a kind of miracle. That is, even abstracted from its content, the form would still be beautiful. A writer can return again and again all through his life to such a model and learn something each time.

Subplotting. The subplot hardly exists in short stories. There the demands of unity and the tight limitations of space require a concentration on the fate of a single character, usually, and at most a concentration on the denouement of one particular situation.

The larger scope of the novel permits some scattering of focus. In novels of blockbuster size—like *War and Peace, Vanity Fair,* or *The Naked and the Dead*—there are very many characters in whose individual destinies we are interested. Here the question is not so much one of subplots as of a number of plots existing side by side in the same enormous work.

In *Madame Bovary,* however, the rise of the pharmacist Homais offers an excellent example of a subplot which remains fairly distinct from the main action—the decline and fall of Emma Bovary—but which contributes a great deal to the thematic statement of the novel. It would be pointless here to try to summarize Flaubert's book and try to show how irony springs from the relation between main plot and subplot. But it is very much to the point to recommend a reading of the novel, and to conclude this chapter with a list of other recommended readings.

If you were enrolled in my writing class and told me you were planning to write a novel, I would ask you to read the following books before you began. As it is, I can only urge that you read them with the same attention you have given to the stories in this volume.

The list was not compiled with the idea that these are the best of contemporary novels. The titles were selected in the same spirit as the stories that are printed here. Purposely I am mentioning few books. It is better, I think, for a writer to know a handful of novels well than to have a sketchy acquaintance with a great many.

The Great Gatsby, F. Scott Fitzgerald. Read this one for its splendid organization, noting particularly the relation between the present dramatic action and the flashbacks that fill in the history of the main characters.

By Love Possessed, James Gould Cozzens. Read for the virtuoso technique in managing several interrelated stories and the management of time. The present action takes place within a three-day period. The past is caught into his action by a splendid variety of flashbacks. Some complications of style are perhaps too much the author's idiosyncrasy to serve as a useful example, but the dialogue is excellent.

The Wild Palms, William Faulkner. Read this as an example of the complex rhetorical novel told in the third person. Study the way tonal effects and melodrama may serve in a serious novel.

The Day of the Locust, Nathaniel West. Note how the novel in a compressed form can serve satiric as well as realistic ends. The style is terse but rich.

Parktilden Village, George P. Elliott. Read this as an example of the contemporary realistic novel at its best. The commonplace scene is made to reveal wonders and horrors through the sharpness of the author's observation. An excellent, clear "middle style" that is worth analysis.

APPENDIX

Appendix

Professional practices. I define professionalism simply as *control*. It is control over the circumstances of writing and the writer's life as well as control of the elements of fiction that make up stories and novels.

The guiding principle for professional writing is to do everything you can the easy way. Writing is hard work. That part of it which counts most is terribly hard. It always will be. Therefore all the practical details connected with the craft ought to be reduced to system and disposed of with minimum effort. No armies are so pitiful as those that spend all their ammunition on the way to the battlefield. Writers who fritter away their best energies from lack of organization belong in the same class.

Writing times and habits. Is it easier for you to force a piece of work out in one sustained burst, skipping meals and drinking black coffee until it is done? Or is it easier to add a little each day, pausing for scrutiny and relaxation between bursts of energy? Do your ideas flow most freely just after you get up in the morning? Or after dinner in the evening? When you first start to work? Or after you have warmed up for an hour or two?

287

The answers to such questions are not going to be the same for any two individuals. The novelist Trollope wrote for a fixed brief period each morning. Balzac locked himself in a small apartment and sweated himself thin until he was ready to come out with a finished novel. As for you, you won't know when you first start writing seriously what your optimum times and conditions are. You must observe yourself a while. But once you get an inkling of the conditions from which your best work emerges, organize the schedule of your life (or your classes, if you are in school) so you can repeat those conditions consistently. And if you find that an hour or two or three in the morning is your best working time, make a point of working *every* morning at that time. There will be periods when writing seems to be no fun at all and you'll need the inertia of habit to keep you going.

As for working conditions, again each individual must measure himself, find where the best comes from the easiest, then try to stabilize those conditions. Don't minimize the importance of even small details.

For instance, some people do their best when they write in longhand, using a dark pencil, and putting no more than a hundred words on each sheet of paper. Others do their best when they compose on a typewriter. Some authors write on only half the sheet, leaving the other half blank for corrections and additions to be made later. Some do their best when they write a first draft at top speed. Others are most effective when they go very slowly, considering each word, and producing a finished work when they put down the last period.

I know a writer who always puts a carbon and a second sheet in his typewriter when he works. This does not mean that he never makes corrections. It means that on those occasional pages that need no corrections he has saved himself the labor of retyping—has saved that much energy to be devoted to more important things.

Is it easiest for you to work after solitude? After you

have been reading for an hour or two? When you have been stimulated by conversation? Some writers find the need for isolating their working hours from the normal concerns of the day by preceding them with a special distraction. For my part I usually work best in the morning after going to a Grade C movie the night before. This is something more than whimsical self-indulgence, and I usually try to arrange such a sequence when I have a very hard bit of work to get done.

Do you work best on an absolutely bare table? Or do you need a clutter of books and notes within grabbing distance? Do you need scratch paper, if you're working on a typewriter, to catch the overflow of ideas you're not yet ready to incorporate into the text of your story?

Well, you must experiment in the beginning. Watch yourself the way you'd watch a laboratory animal. Then adhere to the results of your experiments as they become definite. Organize yourself—but not to the point of mechanical rigidity. One of the things you'll note about yourself, if you observe well, is that, after all, you are a human being, not a machine.

Paper, notebooks, and files. A professional writer respects paper—so he doesn't mind wasting it. The professional is the man who gets things on paper. He knows the difference between "having a great idea" and putting that idea into words on paper. When he hears a bit of dialogue that seems particularly expressive or characteristic, he wants to make sure he understands its quality. The best way to make sure is to try to reproduce it. On paper. As everyone who has made a grocery list should know, the mere mechanical act of putting words on paper fixes them in the memory more durably than they would be fixed by thought alone.

Cultivate the habit of putting things down. Go about the world with pencil and paper in your pocket.

And some of your jottings—not necessarily all of them

—should end in a notebook that you'll keep as a more or less permanent reservoir. A notebook ought to contain (1) ideas for stories, (2) fragments of description, dialogue, and analysis, and (3) quotations from your reading, plus references to titles of works in which you have made some technical, aesthetic, or psychological discovery.

I think the chief value of a writer's notebook is that it serves as a kind of incubator. He catches some partial insight, overhears some news whose significance is not quite clear to him. He has no use for it at the moment. Perhaps he is already busy with a story that claims all his attention. Perhaps the fragment he has caught is too alien to his present experience to be expanded into anything more. In either case, if he puts it in his notebook and leaves it there a while, it may—it just may—hatch a good while later. For one thing, his experience may catch up to the intuition that flared when the notation was made. What was an isolated candle may, in the course of time, be one in a series of illuminations. Its relevance—so dubious when it was put down—may be splendidly obvious.

Files are essential chiefly for storing manuscripts and drafts of manuscripts. Sometimes the very best thing to do with a story when it is finished—when you have utterly exhausted your skill and insight in working on it—is to file it away. It may not be a total success. It may not be publishable. But it is *on paper,* and that, as far as we are concerned, is the main thing. Strange things may happen to your story and you while it remains filed away. When you pull it out of the file after several months or a year, your relation to it will have changed wondrously. In the meantime you will have written other things. Your critical powers as well as your emotional configuration will have altered, and from the vantage point of this alteration you may very well see a possible new dimension to what you considered finished.

Early as well as finished drafts of stories ought to be filed. Sometimes a finished draft has smothered out some vital potentialities of a story that were still struggling to survive in other drafts. When the time comes for a reconsideration of the whole effort, one finds himself ready—as he was not before—to discard the choices that made the final draft and begin again on the lines of an earlier one.

The point of filing, then, is much the same as of keeping a notebook. It permits incubation, ripening. It preserves something on paper while the writer turns his attention to other obligations.

And though I have been talking chiefly of unpublished work, I should say that it is a good idea to keep a file of published work as well. After all, the world of your writing is the world in which your imagination has grown and thrived. Immersing oneself in that world again and again by rereading what you have done in the past is a pretty good way to keep the imagination green. Few of us are tempted to go on with revisions of work once it has been published. But each new work ought, perhaps, to have its roots in what has already been accomplished and ought, in a certain sense, to represent a revision and an extension of the image of the world we once expressed.

Another very practical reason for filing unpublished and unpublishable manuscripts is that they may, some time, be publishable, with or without revision. Stories that languished in an author's files while his reputation was non-existent or small have more than once been in demand after his reputation was established.

But a final caution needs to be spoken on both note-books and files. They may, all too easily, amount to clutter. Now, some writers thrive in the midst of clutter. Clutter on their desks and on the floor around their desks. Clutter in their minds—a rich cluttered jungle from which they can draw as the occasion of their work demands. Others are simply stifled unless they can burn their debris behind them and go on without encumbrances or the weight of unfinished business. We've all heard of authors who claim they never look again at something they've finished.

The answer here is that you must find what works best for you. Keep a running check on yourself. Find in the course of time whether you are smothered or sustained by the accumulation of paper that bears the words you put on it.

Revision. The amount and extent of revision any story or novel will require depends on (1) luck and (2) the amount of effective struggle that went into the first draft.

The mark of the professional in this respect is purely and simply the *willingness* to revise as often and as thoroughly as is required to give the story its best and proper form. The professional regards fiction as a completely plastic medium, something that can be squeezed, pinched, built up, cut down, drawn thin or rolled fat until the form of words and paragraphs on the page conforms to the inherent meaning of the conception and subject.

Now as the writer advances in experience he will develop certain, more or less flexible, habits of revision. That is, if it is his practice to write a complete first draft at top speed, he will expect to rewrite this draft section by section as a second step. If he prepares the first draft more thoughtfully and painstakingly, he may expect merely to make some interlinear changes, alter a few paragraphs, adjust the proportions, polish the language, and then type out a final draft.

But whatever standard steps he thinks will be required to produce a finished manuscript, he will be constantly ready to expand the effort of revision until he gets what he wants. You can never tell what any particular story will require. One will come out almost effortlessly, like toothpaste squeezed out of a tube. (Sometimes a writer has luck, sometimes the luck runs thin.) Another will prove infinitely obstinate. After the first draft it will appear to require not merely revision but a complete rewriting. After the rewriting it may seem faulty in conception. After the conception is straightened out, it will require another tentative draft. And so on. Sometimes the easy stories turn out best. Sometimes the recalcitrant ones. The professional is willing to serve in either case, like any other professional man—a doctor, perhaps, who is happy if a simple prescription cures but willing to perform surgery all night in case it doesn't.

For whatever it is worth, I'll describe (or confess) the history of composition of most of my short stories.

First I did a reasonably careful draft. The rate of composition was probably a page and a half or two pages an hour, though I found that after very slow beginnings I began to move faster as the shape of the story clarified.

A day or two or a week after this first draft was done, I worked over the manuscript with a pencil. I made some changes of a single word, some changes as extensive as a paragraph in length. Almost always I had to rewrite the beginning extensively for the sake of economy and to make it conform to developments I hadn't foreseen when I began. The endings I had first written were usually too abrupt and had to be modulated and paced better. I found a number of passages that were mere shorthand—clear enough to me, but bound to mystify any other reader. These had to be spelled out more distinctly.

Then I typed what was intended as a final draft. I typed very slowly, making some small changes in language and sentence structure as I went along. (I don't like to give my work to a typist. I like to see the finished pages, one by one, to scrutinize them closely and to do them over if they seem in any way faulty.)

After this draft was done, I submitted the stories for publication. Many of them were repeatedly rejected and so, after about a year or two had passed from the date I thought them finished, I had manuscripts back on my hands.

Then I went seriously to work on revisions. There is

something very gratifying to me about working over a story that has already been built up to a certain point of finish and complexity. The material in my hands seems rich and full of possibilities for both strength and subtlety. So in several cases these delayed revisions resulted in the best stories I have ever done. Some of those that were worked on over a period of years have a depth and resonance quite lacking in their earlier versions.

By now I hope I have overcome most of my impatience to rush my work into print. I understand that some pieces can't be hurried, and where that is the case I hope to let them ripen until they are ready.

A final word on revision. It is to your advantage not to submit a story—either to editors for publication or to an instructor or literary friend for criticism—until you have done everything you can to make it as good as possible. The necessity for subsequent revision should not be "taken for granted." It should be done to the best of your ability before the story leaves your hands.

Preparing the manuscript for submission. Always keep a carbon copy of anything you let go out of your sight.

That is the first rule, applicable from the time you start to write. There should be no exceptions at all. You're to blame if the only existing copy of your work disappears through accident or the thousand and one mischances that may arise when you turn over a manuscript to friend, teacher, or editor.

Manuscripts ought to be neatly typed, double-spaced (always) on one side only of standard sheets of white paper. Allow a reasonable margin. The double-spacing and margin permit notes and corrections to be inserted without making the copy illegible. This is particularly important when manuscript is being prepared for the printer.

Make sure you have a decent ribbon in your typewriter when you prepare a manuscript for submission to an editor. Don't fold the manuscript. In a word, your submission should be as easy to read as you can make it. It's a law of life that editors read fast and are subject to eyestrain. However detached and impartial they may be, they don't like to suffer to find the virtues of your work.

All submissions to magazines should be made with a simple covering letter. It need say no more than that you are submitting your work to be considered for publication. Don't go in for autobiography in such a letter. Tact requires brevity.

Include a stamped, self-addressed envelope with all submissions.

Then—hope patiently for the best.

When should you begin to submit your work for publication? As soon as you have done stories that satisfy you. Don't be afraid to submit if you can afford the postage. Editors are not insulted by submissions, whether they can use them or not, whether they admire them or not.

Don't pay any attention to rejection slips or letters of rejection. (Some young writers spend a great deal of effort trying to read between the lines of rejection slips, taking personally the statements that have no personal application.) When a story comes back rejected, put it in another envelope and send it to another magazine.

Do you need an agent? If you have to ask that question, the answer is probably No. Agents are more useful to established writers than to young ones who are trying to make a place for themselves. An agent's bread and butter comes from arranging favorable contracts for novels and from exploiting his personal contacts with editors in placing the work of authors who consistently make money. While many agents are willing to handle the work of unknown writers, they may handle it in a very haphazard fashion, showing less discrimination in submissions than the writer would have.

If your work is of publishable quality, it is just about

as easy to interest an editor in it as to find an agent who will handle it conscientiously. So why not submit it directly?

Most magazines are as receptive to stories submitted directly by the author as to stories that come from agents. On the other hand a novel submitted by an agent may have a slight edge over one that comes unsolicited through the mail.

How do you go about getting an agent? One way is to publish some fiction. Agents keep an eye out for new writers, and after you have a story or two in print you are likely to hear from one agent or another. Usually they will want to know if you have a novel in progress, since it is apparently only novels that have a chance to make serious money for either writer or agent.

It may be flattering to you that an agent is interested in your work. But don't be too hasty about putting your literary affairs in his hands. And above all, don't be distracted by great expectations just because an agent may be submitting your stories for you. Go on working just as you have been. Nothing counts finally except your own accomplishment. It is all too easy to daydream that agents can magically upgrade your accomplishments or your fortunes.

They can't.

The writer's life. I'll end these notes on professionalism with some half-serious comments on the most serious subject of all. Of course the way a writer organizes his life has everything to do with the frustration or the flourishing of his talents.

The way he makes his living, the way he marries, and the way he commits his future are all factors that will condition his success as a writer.

It is not easy to earn a living by writing fiction. Very few people in these United States do it. It takes some recklessness on the part of the young to anticipate a career as professional writer. I'd never take it on my shoulders to advise anyone to try.

And yet I know—you know it too—that without a salting of recklessness life may not be worth living. It is not necessarily prudent to stifle or smother a talent just because following it involves grave risks. Practical people don't throw their lives away, and if writing should be your life then immeasurable sacrifices are justified in going on as a writer.

Usually this isn't the case. Most of us can find some decent compromise between the requirements of society and the requirements of our work. It is generally true that the better the writer the more common sense he has. And it is to common sense that you must look for decisions about a career.

Common sense will oblige you to take stock every now and then of your progress and your chances. It may be that in spite of interest and industry you are not cut out to be a writer who earns a name and a wage by writing fiction. It would be folly to go on year after year sacrificing to a talent too small to pay back the investment.

But if common sense tells you this is the case, you need not believe for one minute that all the effort and the hope you have thus far poured into the task of writing have been wasted.

Whatever you have gained of insight into life and into the creative process will be a permanent possession. And nothing obliges you to stop writing just because you decide not to make a career of it.

You have a craft that is far more than a hobby. You have a means of self-education that is far more than a do-it-yourself program for self-improvement.

To the extent that you have learned to control the art of fiction you have earned the right to consider yourself a professional. You have within your power the means to enrich and humanize all the vicissitudes that life can bring you. Cherish it and extend it.

If, on the other hand, common sense, hard common sense, tells you once and tells you again that you have no good choice in this world except to go hell for leather toward a career in writing, then God bless you.

Marry as a writer.

Eat as a writer.

Drink as a writer.

Make friends as a writer.

Grieve as a writer.

Go in debt as a writer.

Work, work, work, as a writer.

Play as a writer.

Choose writer's illnesses.

Vote as a writer.

Keep physically fit for the sake of writing.

Rejoice as a writer.

And—win, lose, or draw in your ambitions—give thanks for the art you are privileged to practice.

A LIST

of

PUBLISHERS

A List of Publishers

Below, under numeral I are listed most of the publishers of hardcover books who would be receptive to novel manuscripts. Under numeral II you will find a selected list of magazines publishing short stories. As you will realize, some of these magazines have very large circulations, while some of the literary reviews print fewer than a thousand copies of each issue. Payment for fiction varies considerably. It is a good idea to know something of the character of a magazine before you submit stories to it.

In all cases send return envelopes and postage with your submissions.

I

Appleton-Century-Crofts, 60 E. 42nd St., New York
Atheneum Publishers, 162 E. 38th St., New York 16
Atlantic Monthly Press,
    8 Arlington St., Boston 16, Mass.
The Bobbs-Merrill Company, Inc.,
    1720 E. 38th St., Indianapolis 6, Ind.

Citadel Press, 222 Park Avenue S., New York 3
The Dial Press, Inc., 461 Park Avenue S., New York 16
Doubleday & Company, Inc.,
    575 Madison Avenue, New York
Duell, Sloan & Pearce, 60 E. 42nd St., New York
E. P. Dutton & Company, Inc.,
    300 Park Avenue S., New York 10
Harcourt, Brace & World, Inc.,
    750 Third Avenue, New York 17
Harper & Row, 49 E. 23rd St., New York 16
Holt, Rinehart & Winston, Inc.,
    383 Madison Avenue, New York 17
Alfred A. Knopf, Inc., 501 Madison Ave., New York 22
Little, Brown & Company,
    34 Beacon St., Boston 6, Mass.
McGraw-Hill Book Company, Inc.,
    330 W. 42nd St., New York
The Macmillan Company, 60 Fifth Ave., New York 11
Ivan Obolensky, Inc., 341 E. 62nd St., New York 21
Pantheon Books, Inc., 333 Sixth Ave., New York 14
G. P. Putnam's Sons, 200 Madison Ave., New York
Random House, Inc., 457 Madison Ave., New York 22
Henry Regnery Company, Reilly & Lee Co.,
    14 E. Jackson Blvd., Chicago 4, Ill.
Charles Scribner's Sons, 597 Fifth Ave., New York 17
Simon and Schuster, Inc., 630 Fifth Ave., New York 20
The Viking Press, Inc., 625 Madison Ave., New York 22

II

Antioch Review, Antioch College, Yellow Springs, Ohio
Argosy, 205 E. 42nd St., New York 17
Arizona Quarterly,
    311 Library, The University of Arizona, Tucson,
    Arizona
Atlantic Monthly, 8 Arlington St., Boston 16, Mass.

Carolina Quarterly, Box 1117, Chapel Hill, N. C.

Chicago Review,
> Box A, Faculty Exchange, University of Chicago, Chicago 37, Ill.

The Colorado Quarterly,
> Hellems 118, University of Colorado, Boulder, Colo.

Cosmopolitan, 57th St. at Eighth Ave., New York 19

Epoch,
> 159 Goldwin Smith, Cornell University, Ithaca, New York

Esquire, 488 Madison Ave., New York 22

Fantasy and Science Fiction,
> 580 Fifth Ave., New York 36

Georgia Review, University of Georgia, Athens, Ga.

Good Housekeeping,
> 57th St. at Eighth Ave., New York 19

The Grecourt Review,
> Smith College, Northampton, Mass.

Harper's Bazaar, 572 Madison Ave., New York 22

Harper's Magazine, 49 E. 33rd St., New York 16

Hudson Review, 65 E. 55th St., New York 22

The Kenyon Review,
> Kenyon College, Gambier, Ohio

Ladies' Home Journal,
> Independence Square, Philadelphia 5, Pa.

The Literary Review,
> Fairleigh Dickinson University, Teaneck, N. J.

Mademoiselle, 575 Madison Ave., New York 22

McCall's, 230 Park Ave., New York 17

Minnesota Review,
> Box 4068, University Station, Minneapolis 14, Minn.

Mutiny, Box 278, Northport, N. Y.

The New Yorker, 25 W. 43rd St., New York 36

Northwest Review, University of Oregon, Eugene, Ore.

The Paris Review, 45-39 171 Place, Flushing 58, N. Y.

Playboy, 232 E. Ohio, Chicago 11, Ill.
Prairie Schooner, 105 Andrews Hall, Lincoln, Nebraska
The Saturday Evening Post,
      Independence Square, Philadelphia 5, Pa.
Seventeen, 320 Park Ave., New York 22
The Sewanee Review,
      University of the South, Sewanee, Tenn.
Southwest Review,
      Southern Methodist University, Dallas 22, Texas
Virginia Quarterly Review,
      1 West Range, Charlottesville, Va.